Please note that this book is written as a thought-provoking instrument to help you decide to pursue further financial knowledge. I do not offer advice in this book to you on making specific investments. Please seek advice from licensed financial advisors and tax accountants should you decide to put any investment or tax ideas into practice. I am in no way responsible for your gains or losses should you choose to pursue any investments.

MINDSET TO MILLIONS

Building Your Empire to Financial Freedom

Brian Carruthers

MINDSET TO MILLIONS

Published by Pinnacle Press

Editing, cover design, and layout by Paul Braoudakis

www.briancarruthers.com

ISBN: 978-1-7331906-6-4

Printed in the United States of America

PINNACLE PRESS

CONTENTS

ACKNOWLEDGMENTS

There are two ways we can learn to build wealth: by having great, wealthy mentors who are willing to teach us what they have learned, or by learning through trial and error on our own. Many people do not seek mentorship; instead, they choose to navigate the financial journey on their own and pray for the best. I knew from an early age that it was best to seek help from those who have what you want. So I must thank the mentors in my life, both personal and at a distance. Nobody came knocking on my door to force their advice on me. I went knocking, and a few mentors opened their doors to me. I went into my learning with a very open mind, and I made sure to apply everything I could.

Thank you to my parents for being such amazing role models for managing their money wisely. Growing up, I watched them build large businesses and amass great fortunes. Although we had everything we needed and wanted, they were also quite frugal. I learned so much from them about how to treat and respect money. The legacy they will leave behind is far greater than bank accounts and assets. They passed on a legacy of a wealth mindset. It is extremely important for me to live in the same way, and in turn pass on that mindset to my own family. My sons will be the beneficiaries of all that I have learned.

To Paul J Meyer, who spent personal time with me, helped me to think bigger about building wealth and making my work my ministry. I learned that my mission cannot be just about my own financial goals; it should also include helping many others change their lives, too. To whom much is given, much is expected. My mission in life is to empower people financially and to pass along the principles and strategies I have learned to the willing.

To my fellow wealth builders, I urge you to slow down to speed up. Take the time to lay a solid foundation of sound financial philosophies before running out there to conquer the world. Build your empires on solid ground so that no tremor can bring you down. All the money in the world will do you no good if you are loading it into a box riddled with holes. Your money mindset should be your foremost concern. Let me help you the way some of my mentors helped me. Take me with you, and always refer back to the mindset in this book to guide your financial decisions. I look forward to seeing you build your wealth to a level you have never imagined possible.

In this updated edition, I'd also like to acknowledge the evolving landscape of finance since the original publication in 2015. The rise of digital tools, AI-driven investing, and sustainable practices has transformed how we build wealth. Thanks to modern fintech innovators and the global community of entrepreneurs who continue to share knowledge through platforms like podcasts, online forums, and social media. Their insights have inspired new sections in this re-release, reminding us that learning never stops. To my readers who have applied these principles and shared their success stories, your feedback has been invaluable in making this book more robust and relevant for today's world.

INTRODUCTION

I fell in love with entrepreneurship and business opportunities and saw how innovative business models can change lives. I saw people use leverage and create incomes they had never seen before. It was revolutionary! But as time went on, I saw things that bothered me to my core. I felt the pain when I saw friends who were mismanaging their newfound money. I saw them blowing money as if there were some guarantee that their income would always grow and flow forever. New cars, new homes, new clothes, wristwatches, first-class flying, fancy vacations, and all types of other splurges became their world.

But this wild-horse nature of unbridled spending behavior almost always caught up to them. Their spending continued to outpace their earnings, and though they had money, they were just broke at a higher level. Or something would happen beyond their control, and they were caught unprepared. Perhaps the company they were building in had problems, or some team members left, and they lost sales volume, or the economy had taken a bad turn. The next thing you know, their income is cut in half. They were losing their cars and homes. They were behind on paying taxes. In effect, their lives were flipped upside down.

Why did this happen? In a word (or two): *Wrong mindset.* This scenario is indicative of what happens when people find a way to make money but don't have the right mindset or plan to handle the money they are making. I feel a deep joy when I see an individual achieving financial success, as a huge smile spreads from ear to ear. I love knowing that their financial stress is being relieved, and that they are living a richer life than they ever knew before. But on the flip side, when things turn, I feel the pain inside knowing how this shocking surprise rocks their world.

This is why I had to write this book.

My first book, *Making My First Ten Million,* was written to inspire people to pursue business opportunities. My second book, *Building an Empire,* was written to teach how to build a business from scratch and achieve significant income. My third book, *Untrapped,* helped people stuck in the 9-5 hamster wheel think bigger and start their own businesses. I am excited that those books have been wildly successful in accomplishing those goals. But now that so many people are making incredible incomes, I feel an obligation to talk about how to manage your money wisely.

Now, there may be critics who might knock this book for not being a detailed 300-page tome on stock investing or a thorough treatise on tax accounting for home-based business owners. But please hear me, that is *not* what this book is about. This book is about *mindset*. It is about thinking differently regarding money and wealth, so that you will have an inflamed desire to pursue further knowledge on all such subjects. I can tell you that what I write about here is exactly what has served me very, very well throughout my life. While I am not a CPA, certified financial planner, or even an expert stock investor, the principles you are about to absorb have created a level of wealth that provides me with great financial peace and security.

Let's begin the conversation assuming many readers are currently in debt and just beginning to develop a plan to achieve financial independence. Of course, I expect that some readers might already have a great plan and are further along in their quest to build wealth. Frankly, since a wise person is never done learning, some readers may be further along than I am. But in any case, if you are reading this, it means you want to do better. You want every advantage you can stack in your favor.

Since the original edition, the world has seen unprecedented economic shifts — from the 2020 pandemic's impact on global markets to the rise of digital currencies and AI in finance.

This re-release builds on those timeless principles with new insights into resilience, technology, and sustainable investing. We've added sections on side hustles, inflation protection, and legacy planning to make this guide even more comprehensive for today's readers facing inflation rates around 2.7 percent, unemployment at 4.4 percent, and household debt exceeding $18.6 trillion. These updates aim to equip you not just for wealth building but for thriving in an ever-changing financial landscape. Let's dive in with fresh eyes on what it means to master money in today's economic climate.

So here we go.

THE MONEY MINDSET

Money is a very, very powerful thing. It is a force that moves the world. People will work all day for it, steal and cheat for it, lie awake at night because they don't have enough of it, and change others' lives by giving it away. Many people live their lives as slaves to money, while others are the masters of money. If you want to be a master of money, you must first develop an understanding of money, a respect for it, and an appreciation of it.

Understand it. Respect/appreciate it. Attract it. Make it. Keep it. Control it. Grow it. Impact others with it.

Before we can truly delve into developing our money mindset, it makes sense to try and define what mindset is really all about. There are several "official" definitions of mindset, ranging from Webster's "A mental inclination, tendency, or habit," to Oxford's "The established set of attitudes held by someone."

There are several others as well, but all you really need to understand are two things: 1) A mindset is a way of thinking, and 2) Mindset really matters.

According to Carol S. Dweck, the author of *Mindset: The New Psychology of Success: How We Can Learn to Fulfill Our Potential*, there are two kinds of mindsets — a fixed mindset and a growth mindset. On her website, she defines both.

> In a **fixed mindset**, people believe their basic qualities, such as intelligence or talent, are fixed traits. They spend their time documenting their intelligence or talent instead of developing it. They also believe that talent alone creates success — without effort. They're wrong.
>
> In a **growth mindset**, people believe that their most basic abilities can be developed through dedication and hard work — brains and talent are just the starting point. This view fosters a love of learning and resilience, both essential for great accomplishment. Virtually all great people have had these qualities.

Needless to say, we will focus heavily in this book on the *growth mindset* since we are trying to grow ourselves, our incomes, and our businesses to greater levels. Throughout this book, we will assess your current philosophies about money (your fixed mindset) and guide you toward a place where money just seems to find its way to you for the rest of your life (your growth mindset).

Who we are is what we attract. Get ready for some mental shifts.

(Expanded addition: In the decade since a parallel version of this book was first published, mindset research has evolved further, incorporating insights from neuroscience and behavioral economics. Studies from institutions like Stanford and Harvard show that a growth mindset not only boosts financial success but also resilience during economic downturns, such as the 2020 recession. For instance, individuals with a growth mindset are 25 percent more likely to recover from financial setbacks by viewing them as learning opportunities rather than failures. We'll draw on these modern findings to make your transformation even more actionable, including practical exercises like daily affirmations and visualization techniques tailored to today's digital age.)

How Did We Get Here?

It is important to know that you will not transform your financial situation overnight. Where you are financially today is the aggregate result of the decisions you have made over the last 5-10 years of your life — decisions driven by your philosophies and your relationship with money. As famed author and business coach Jim Rohn taught, "You can change your life in any five years. From age 35 to 40, age 23 to 28, age 59 to 64." Just as you should not expect to get rich quick overnight, you also should not expect to become a financial wizard overnight, either.

But the fact that you are reading this book sets you apart from and ahead of 90 percent of the population.

Even small changes in your mindset and actions, done consistently over an extended period of time, can transform you. Darren Hardy of *Success* magazine calls it "The Compound Effect." You are either making the correct little decisions every day, or you are making little judgment errors that, compounded over time, will make or break you. In life and in finances, you either exercise self-discipline, or the world will discipline you. Either way, you will be disciplined. So the point is to set your expectations properly. Expect that this will be a journey ... but one that is worth it if you value getting wealthy.

If you were to study *wealthy* people and study *poor* people as I have, you would find that they are very different. But to find out why, we must look beneath the difference in their bank accounts, the cars they drive, or their spending habits. These are all merely symptoms of their mindsets and philosophies about money. How people feel about money, and even how they feel about whether they are deserving of abundance in their lives, will dictate whether they will attract wealth or repel it. Poor people mostly feel they are undeserving and that money is not good. They sometimes even despise those who have created wealth. They will claim that money is not important, all the while they live with high levels of stress because they do not have the financial resources to afford the cost of living. After years of living with this philosophy, they become accustomed to a life of lack and oppression.

Broke is different than poor. Broke is temporary. I have studied many people with the right mindset and philosophies, but they were either working on their wealth or in between winning streaks. Just because their bank account was at zero, that didn't mean they were poor. They had the wealthy mindset and were working on attracting and creating the results. Putting politics aside, before he became president, Donald Trump was worth over a *billion* dollars. But for years during a real estate downturn, his business ventures were hit hard, and he found himself in personal debt of over $900 million. People complain about having no money all the time, but can you imagine being underwater by $900 million? But Donald Trump was never poor. Poor is a state of mind, and he always had the wealth mindset even when he was down. And it was his mindset (and work ethic and skills) that saw him back to the top — *Forbes* magazine estimates his current net worth at more than $5 billion, and the *New York Times* says it's closer to $10 billion. Because he was never poor, he became unbroke.

Today, with U.S. household debt at around $18.6 trillion and student loan debt at $1.8 trillion, many more people find themselves "broke" due to systemic factors such as inflation and job-market shifts. But mindset remains the differentiator. Recent studies from the Federal Reserve show that individuals with a growth mindset are 30 percent more likely to climb out of debt cycles by seeking education and side opportunities. To apply this, try a simple exercise: Track your daily financial thoughts for a week. Note negative patterns (e.g., "I'll never get ahead") and reframe them (e.g., "I'm building skills to create abundance"). This practice, backed by cognitive behavioral therapy research, can accelerate your shift from scarcity to prosperity thinking.)

Stay The Course

I ask you, up front, to stay with me as we take this journey together. You may want to run ahead if you feel like you are reading something you already know. But I believe you cannot get the desired result if you decide to skip parts of this wealth mindset-building process. *How* to make the money and what to do with the money — these are the easier components to learn. But you do not want to build your financial structure on sand. So we must drill really deep and lay an extremely solid foundation first. The deeper the foundation, the bigger your financial empire can be built upon it. The good news is you've already found the *how*: Through incredible business models like entrepreneurship. You discovered the better way to get ahead financially, and have committed to this path (at least part-time) to create wealth and freedom. I have watched many thousands of people choose this vehicle to be their income-producing machine as they exited the rat race of living check to check and chasing money indefinitely.

Personally, I believe the most powerful kind of money comes from passive income. This usually involves a business that pays you overrides on the sales made by others and the lifetime residual income stream from your customer base. For those who have discovered it, however, this is where most entrepreneurs' vision ends. They make money, and they spend it just as quickly. If you're fortunate enough to tap into this source of income — or *any* significant source of income — it is vital that you have specific plans for what to do with it so you arrive where you desire in the next five years.

Let's get your mind thinking about going to the next level. You've heard the sayings, "It takes money to make money," and "The rich keep getting richer." These statements do hold truths, but only for the educated and disciplined. Your business is the cash machine. You must have the intent to build wealth rather than spend your money. You must learn how to legally keep as much of what you earn as you can. Then the ultimate goal is to learn how to invest; how to put overalls on your money and have it go to work for you. The end game should be for you to be able to live your life off the interest income from your investments without ever touching the principle. For example, my goal was to create enough cash flow from my business to invest $10 million, which at just 5 percent interest, would generate $500,000 a year for me to live on — without ever having to touch the $10 million. Can you imagine?

Most people want to jump right into asking about what investments they should put their monies into. That is not the right question ... yet. We first must establish the right mindset. Without this as a foundation, you can never get to the destination of financial freedom. Sadly, 95 percent of the population does not have this mindset. Once your thinking about money is right, then we can get into how to keep the money that you earn. This will address your spending habits, as well as business expenses and paying taxes. Next, we can determine some strategies for investing what you have kept, so you can watch your money compound and grow. Lastly, in the end, this is what matters most: you can find ways to use your wealth to help others and change the world.

With economic volatility from AI-driven job displacements and persistent inflation, staying the course means more than persistence — it's about adaptability. Modern tools like robo-advisors can help track progress automatically, sending alerts if you're veering off. Add a weekly "mindset check-in" ritual: review your goals, celebrate small wins, and adjust to new realities, such as rising mortgage interest rates. This keeps the journey engaging and resilient against setbacks.)

The Love of Money ...

The first place to start is to examine your personal relationship with money. How do you consciously think about money? And even deeper, how were you conditioned and programmed to *feel* about money throughout your life? Many people have never stopped to ask themselves these important questions.

Ask yourself if you've ever heard these statements:

"The love of money is the root of all evil."

"Money can't buy you happiness."

"Rich people take advantage of others."

"It's not good to be greedy, so money is not important."

"The love of money is bad."

If you were raised in an environment where you heard such things, you are likely *repelling* money from you instead of *attracting* it to you — and you don't even realize it. Think about it. If your subconscious deems money intrinsically bad or evil, it will not want you to have it. Consciously, however, in the real world of bills and expenses, you know you need money to live. You have likely worked hard, almost as a slave to money, your entire life. You never really thought of money as a good thing, but rather a necessary evil in life.

When your mind deems something as "evil," it tends to repel it. For instance, if you ingest contaminated food or something poisonous, your conscious mind need not even be triggered. An unconscious message is sent to your body to throw it up, to rid your body of that which is bad or could hurt you. In the same way, your environment has wired or programmed you to act in this same way with regard to money. If money is bad or evil, you will find ways to get rid of it as fast as you earn it. Thus, it is next to impossible for you to ever grow your wealth.

Another example of how a physical disdain for money can manifest in your relationship with money can be found in a recent study, "How 'Dirty' Money Affects Spending Behavior." In a paper titled "Money Isn't Everything, But it Helps if it

Doesn't Look Used: How the Physical Appearance of Money Influences Spending," professor Theodore Noseworthy called it the "Ick Factor."

"We tend not to like money that looks like a lot of others have touched it," Noseworthy says. "People want to get rid of worn currency because they're disgusted by the contamination of others." He adds, "Where someone with a crisp bill would tend to hold onto it ... someone with a worn bill tends to use it as soon as they get it."

So whether it's your brain expelling poison from your body to keep you healthy, or your getting rid of dirty money due to subconscious disgust, these are very strong parallels to your own personal relationship with money. Take a moment now to evaluate your money mindset. If you have always had trouble attracting money or keeping what you have earned, I am confident you will remember hearing the negative programming about money earlier in your life. The good news is that you can reprogram your mind starting now. You can attract money into your life. To do this, you must swing to the other side of the spectrum. You can learn to love money.

Read this aloud right now: **"I LOVE MONEY!"**

How did that feel? Did that cause you to feel uneasy? Would you be afraid that people might judge you if they heard you say this? How would your friends or family label you for saying this? Does this fear maybe keep you from gaining wealth? It is important for each of us to recognize that we all seek acceptance, love, and respect from others. If others think of money as evil, of course, we wouldn't want to speak against their moral truths. So how do we deal with this? We must create our own new truths. Then we can better deal with the outside world that would rather have us join them in the normal and familiar, yet uncomfortable state of lack.

You see, I don't love money itself. But I do love what money can do as a tool in life. I really do. And because I love that having money can be used to bless my life and those around me, I seek it, and I attract it. But let me explain how I think and what my mindset is all about.

Money is not paper nor piles of gold. Money is a means of exchange of value, a means to an end. So when I say, "I love money as a tool," what I am really saying is "I love what money can do." Money is not bad or good, in and of itself. The greed of it, or doing bad things for or with money, is where bad can creep in. More money will simply make you more of what you already are. If you were a jerk before you had money, you'll just be a richer jerk. Money won't make you a better person. Conversely, if you were a good and giving person before you had money, you'll be an even better and more giving person now that you have it.

Here are a few questions to help you learn to love what money can do:

» Assume someone in your family became very ill and she needed advanced medical care to save her life. But this treatment was only available overseas and the cost was going to be into the hundreds of thousands. How much would you love to pull out your checkbook and handle it altogether? Would you love it?

» Your son wants to attend a private school in town because it offers the best programs for his interests. But tuition for this school is more than $20,000 a year. How great would it feel to go into his bedroom one night and say, "Honey, we are going to let you go to the school of your dreams"? Wouldn't you love that?

» Every Sunday, your church shows how much it's trying to raise to fulfill the budget for mission trips and community outreach programs for those in need. You can see that the budget is $22,000 behind. Wouldn't you love to be able to drop in on the pastor on Monday and hand him a check for that amount with a big smile on your heart? Wouldn't you love that?

» Your parents haven't driven a new car in almost 15 years. Times are tight, and the car just isn't what you want them to be driving. How amazing would it feel to have them walk out of their front door one day to find a gorgeous new car parked in their driveway, with a huge red bow across the hood, and "I love you, Mom and Dad!" written across the windshield? Wouldn't you love that?

- The economy dives into recession. Jobs are being lost, and people can't afford to keep their homes. The stock market is crashing, and people's 401(k)s are cut in half overnight. Wouldn't you love the peace of mind that comes from knowing you created a financial moat around you and your family that can endure even such a deep economic downturn?

Can you find all sorts of things to fall in love with based on what money can do for you? I decided early in life to associate the goodness in these things with the concept of money itself. These things I love have made me want money. We attract that which we want and think about. If I love the things and blessings I can bestow, I can attach better emotions to that which will make these things possible. I didn't start off enjoying reading books. It was quite tiring for me. I would fall asleep after reading 20 pages, or have to go back and re-read an entire page because I hadn't absorbed what I had just read. But I loved what I got from reading, so now I tell people I love reading.

With this understanding, say this aloud: **"I LOVE THAT HAVING MONEY WILL HELP ME DO SO MUCH GOOD!"**

How did that feel this time? I expect this new psychological underpinning will make you feel differently about these words. The more you say them to yourself and think deeply beneath the surface, the better your relationship with money will become. You attract what you think about most often. So think good thoughts about money going forward, and think often. Money is something your unconscious thoughts can help you *magnetize.*

You've heard the saying, "Money can't buy happiness," right? Well, neither can *brokenness* — yes, I realize that isn't a real word, but the point still stands. Let's be honest: many of life's problems are easier to deal with when you have money rather than when you don't. Money gives you options. It gives you flexibility. You can still be wealthy and unhappy, of course, but it's a lot easier to pursue happiness when financial stress isn't constantly weighing on you.

Here's a simple test. You only get one choice: if you had to live your life with either an abundance of money or very little money, which would you choose? Since your goal is to live a happy life, you just chose the path you believe would make that easier. And most people would answer the same way: "Give me the money." So learn to be at peace with the desire to have plenty of financial resources in your life.

With social media amplifying stories of instant wealth (e.g., viral influencers or crypto millionaires), it's easier than ever to fall into negative money narratives like "wealth is for the lucky" or "rich people are selfish." But research from psychologists like Sonja Lyubomirsky shows that positive affirmations, like the one above, can rewire neural pathways for abundance thinking, increasing financial decision-making by up to 20 percent. To make this practical, try a 30-day challenge: Journal one "money love" story daily — how funds enabled a positive outcome in your life or others'. Combine this with apps that track gratitude for financial wins, turning abstract concepts into tangible habits for lasting mindset change.

THE WEALTH-BUILDING MINDSET

W*ealth* is a noun, while *rich* is an adjective. If someone says, "I am rich," this means their life is filled with blessings or trappings of success. It is wonderful for someone to want to become rich, as long as it does not cloud their value system or the vision of who they are. Wealth is a thing — a measurement of time. Wealth is the length of time you can sustain your accustomed standard of living (expenses) without needing to acquire more money to pay for it.

For example, if your monthly cost of living is $5,000 and you have $100,000 in the bank, then your wealth is 20 months' worth of expenses. This means you could continue living your life without new income for 20 months before your well runs dry. Would you feel wealthy in this scenario? Probably not.

Heaven forbid you lose your job tomorrow, and you cannot find work. You would be out on the street in less than two years. That fear would leave a person feeling insecure. And security is an important human drive. We all want it. So to me, true wealth is having enough money to live comfortably and securely for the balance of your years on earth, even without working to earn another dollar.

With average life expectancies pushing past 80 years and healthcare costs soaring — projected to reach $6.8 trillion annually in the U.S. — true wealth must account for longevity risks like outliving your savings. Tools like retirement calculators (e.g., from Vanguard or Fidelity apps) can help estimate this: Input your age, expected lifespan, inflation (around 2.7 percent), and returns (aim for 7-10 percent post-inflation). This isn't just math; it's mindset — shifting from "surviving" to "thriving" in later years, perhaps by incorporating longevity annuities or health savings accounts for tax-advantaged medical expenses.

How Much Money Will You Need?

Have you created a budget for yourself? Do you know how much you will need to have put away to be able to retire? Forget about all the travel and the fun stuff we tell ourselves we're going to do when we retire. Let's look at just eating:

Let's assume you and your spouse want to retire at 65, and expect to live for 20 years. Let's say the two of you want to eat three times a day, and you want to do so all 365 days of the year. Let's calculate based on a mere $7 per meal.

Two people x 20 years x 365 days x three meals x $7 dollars = $306,600.

You would need to have more than $300,000 in the bank ... just to be able to eat! This assumes you don't live longer than 20 years. This financial scenario allows no money for gas, utilities, insurance, golf, holiday presents for the grandkids, clothes, or medicine — just food! And no eating out ... that would be too expensive!

How much is in your bank account right now? Is it greater than, or less than $306,600?

If your number is far away from this estimate, we've got some work to do. The good news is, you can do it! It will take determination and focus. We will decide now to earn more, spend less, and invest more. We will get you to retirement with the wealth you need.

Adjusting for current realities, with food inflation at 2-3 percent annually and average meal costs now closer to $10-12 due to supply chain issues, that $306,600 figure balloons to over $450,000 when factored for 30 years of retirement (as lifespans extend). Use online calculators like those from

NerdWallet or Bankrate, inputting current data to personalize. To build this, consider automating contributions to Roth IRAs, which grow tax-free. This isn't just numbers — it's empowerment, turning vague retirement dreams into a concrete, achievable roadmap.

New Earners and Their Quandary

In some industries, we are drawn to the stories of people earning big money, traveling the world, driving exotic cars, and posing for the camera in front of their mansions. The flashy trappings of success are supposed to prove that this business is successful and insinuate that they, too, can have all of this.

But we must all realize this is a slippery slope. In many ways, it's a trap.

I have watched all too many new earners living way above their means. On the outside, they look dazzling and happy. But when they log onto their computer at night and look at their online bank statement, the smile disappears. On the inside, many are toiling, restless, and scared. Eventually, this leads people to make poor decisions out of desperation rather than smart ones born of peace of mind and confidence. You will see new earners who cannot stay put in one company long enough to build wealth because their spending-habituated desperation causes them to look for the next shiny object to rescue them.

The sad reality is that on any given day, I can show you two different people who are currently making $50,000 a year from their business venture ... but in five years, one will be broke, while the other has built a sizable net worth. Sad, but true.

MINDSET NUGGETS

"If you will live like no one else, later you can live like no one else."

– ***Dave Ramsey***

If you want to lose weight, you can eat less or work out more. But if you want to get even better results faster, you can eat less and work out more! A similar law applies in wealth building. If you want to build wealth, you can spend less or earn more. But if you want to get there faster, you can spend less *and* earn more!

You can't always control *how much* you earn, but even without earning more, you can immediately control your spending and what you do with the surplus money (more on this later). You're always going to keep working to grow your income. But if income growth is your only focus, you may just end up earning more and still be broke at a higher level. There's nothing gained by earning $100,000 a year and spending $100,000 a year. Actually, all you'll have done is raise the bar on your expenses and skewed your wealth calculation, leaving you with fewer years to live off your savings. So it is imperative that you get these first two topics under control right off the bat.

With gig economy platforms like Uber or Upwork enabling side hustles, new earners face even more temptations — easy access to credit via apps like Affirm or Afterpay fuels impulse buys. A 2025 Federal Reserve survey shows 40 percent of Americans couldn't cover a $400 emergency, highlighting the quandary. To navigate, track "lifestyle creep" with apps like Mint; set rules like delaying purchases 30 days. This builds discipline, turning short-term gains into long-term security.

Spending

Live below your means. This is the easiest way to frame my advice. Whatever amount of income you have coming in, live on less than that. I cannot make it any simpler. When in doubt, just revert to that rule. Truly wealthy people live below their means. Take a look at Warren Buffett, one of the top three wealthiest people in the entire world with a $63 billion net worth. As of this writing, he is still living in the same house he bought for $31,500 in 1958. He doesn't drive a super expensive car, either. He doesn't need to impress anyone, and you can see the peace of mind and heart all over his gentle, smiling face.

Buffett once shared that success has nothing to do with the house you live in. There are many ways someone can measure or define success, but the size of your house really shouldn't have anything to do with it. While life will have its ups and downs, it's the continuous learning, thinking for yourself, developing good habits, focusing on the long term, and having fun on the journey that will set you up for success.

Too often, we get caught up with celebrities on television who are glorified for their mansions, exotic cars, jewelry, and jet-set lifestyle. If you let yourself idolize such people, it is inevitable that you will try to keep up with them in your own proportionate way. This is a recipe for disaster. In fact, many of these clowns lose most or all of the money they earn because they never took the time to learn how to adopt a wealth-building mindset in the first place.

This is why I am so excited you are reading this book. We are going to ensure you keep the wealth you create so you can pass it on and/or bless the world around you with it.

With social media influencers showcasing luxury on TikTok and Instagram, spending pressure is amplified — U.S. consumer debt hit $1.14 trillion, with credit card debt alone totaling $1.14 trillion. Counter this with "conscious consumption": Before buying, ask if it aligns with long-term goals. Tools like budgeting apps (e.g., YNAB) categorize spending, revealing leaks. Remember, true wealth is freedom, not flash — emulate Buffett's frugality for sustained peace.

Disposable Income — There's No Such Thing!

Let's talk about spending habits. This topic is more than just refraining from buying expensive homes and cars. It pervades our daily lives in much smaller transactions. We are talking about developing a new mindset about what things cost, and creating a mental framework for deciding whether the cost of something is worth robbing from your future wealth to pay for it.

Every dollar we spend has an "opportunity cost" attached to it. The *Rule of Seven* means that money invested at a 10 percent compounded rate of return will double every seven years. With this as a constant backdrop in your mind, think about what that $1,000 flat-screen TV really costs. Right now, it's $1,000 cash (assuming you aren't going down the debt rabbit hole and using a credit card). But had you invested that money, in seven years it would have grown to $2,000. In seven more years, it would have been $4,000. So if you have a child right now who is 4 years old, and you hope to pay for his/her college when they turn 18, that $1,000 TV stole $4,000 from your child's education. So the decision-making process has changed for you. A pack of gum isn't $1.50, but rather $3 ... or even $4.50!

Now I don't want to turn your life into one of a miserly existence. But I do want to instill the practice of conscientious thought before you part with your hard-earned money ... and even more so when your money seems not so hard-earned, especially if you have passively flowing income from team overrides while your business is in a momentum phase.

Here is a key topic that ties right in with the opportunity cost discussion. There are many things we spend money on in our daily lives that we could choose not to buy, and instead divert those funds toward investments. Take, for example, a fancy cup of coffee that costs $5. Did you need that expensive cup, or could you have brewed your own for less than a dollar? Or it could be a $6 pack of cigarettes. Or maybe even the extra premium channels in your cable TV package, which add up to $70 a month or more. What if you could find just $10 a day that you could divert from spending and repurpose it into investing in your future? As these bits and pieces add up and then compound interest kicks in to grow it at a 10 percent annual return, look at the graph below to see what happens.

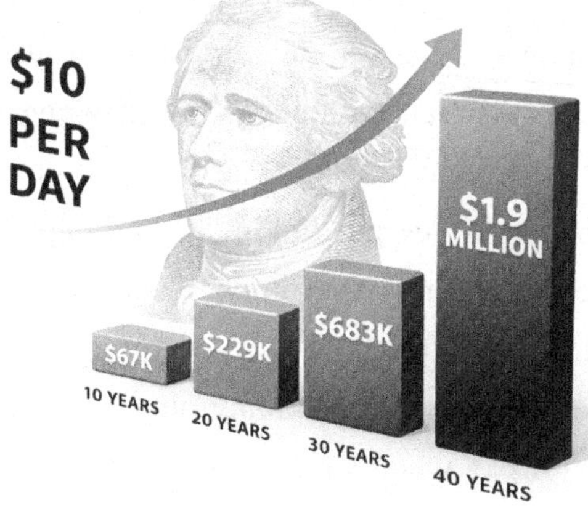

As you can see, every little bit helps. Every dollar compounds. This conversation doesn't even factor in the extra earnings you can invest. We are only starting with some things you currently spend money on that you may be able to cut out. It might be saying no to one last $12 martini at closing time. It might be flying coach rather than first class. (Even though I make millions, I still choose to fly coach for this reason. Good habits are hard to change!) Maybe you can cancel cable TV for a year and see if you really miss it. You might just become more productive as a by-product while saving money! When I say there is no such thing as "disposable income," I mean that you should intend/plan to invest every dollar you can, rather than dispose of it.

I am sensitive to the fact that in entrepreneurship, your prospects do need to see you as successful. So I do understand that we must invest in our appearance. We need to dress for success. But we need to keep that in check and not go overboard. A few nice-looking suits or dresses will do. Maybe you can reward yourself with a new outfit when you hit a benchmark goal in your business. We do want our car to be clean and modern. We do need to invest in things like dental work if needed, to ensure a clean appearance and hygiene. But when people start buying things with their newfound money, like a typical lottery winner, that bling-bling is the biggest tell that they'll be broke when we run into them 10 years from now. I would bet on it, because the more money they make, the smarter they think they are.

Hear this clearly: Money doesn't make you smarter. As a matter of fact, I am writing this book to help people catch up with their money. After all, *money, like water, seeks its own level.* If you don't grow up to where your money is, it will come right back down to who you are. If you are used to making $30,000 a year, and your business venture shoots you up to $100,000, in due time, you will be back to earning $30,000 if you don't develop a six-figure mindset with regard to financial literacy.

Please don't misunderstand me here. I don't want to make it sound like I'm advocating that you live like a pauper and have no quality of lifestyle. But I don't want to give you a blanket license to live a financially irresponsible life, either. So I *cautiously* mention that you do need to do and have nice things. Eating out on a fun Friday night with your family or significant other, taking a cool vacation during the year, or getting a stunning new pair of shoes ... these things can certainly happen. I am merely suggesting that you make calculated decisions. Later in the book, we will talk about budgets and how to set aside money for life's pleasures. With discipline in tow, as your wealth builds, you can ratchet up the amounts you allow yourself to spend on fun.

Look, I own a Bentley GTC, and at one point I owned a Ferrari Spyder (which I recently sold and gave the money to my church). I am certainly all for you getting to a point when you can justify such luxuries, but ... keep it relative and *in proportion* to your income. For example, when I bought the Ferrari, it cost me *six weeks*' worth of my income. To give you a frame of reference, take six weeks of your income. What kind of car could you buy with that? I got the Ferrari only after my income made it possible for me to feel good about buying it. I spend only a small percentage of my monthly income on the extras in life. I have my fixed costs like house, cars, insurance, kids' tuition, etc., but the bulk of what's left goes into investments. Let me tell you, I sleep well knowing that I have a financial moat around my family.

Why do we buy nice things? I think it's important that we contemplate this question. People spend money on things they need and things they want. It goes without saying that if we *need* something, we need something. If we need gas for our car, or heat for our home, or medicine for our health, of course, that doesn't require much thought. But then we have purchases driven by want, not need. It might be a designer purse we would love to hang on our shoulder, or the gorgeous new convertible we would love to drive around town. These purchases fill a need as well, but a different kind.

As humans, we have a *need* to feel loved, respected, and valued. We feel that people will feel more of these things about us if we are all shined up and have nice material things. It shows people that we worked hard and made it! Quite often, part of the drive for us to work so hard is to prove to the world what we are capable of. If you wear a Rolex watch and people see it, they will know you are a success. If people see me drive my Bentley, without even getting to know me, they'll know I'm the real deal. That's how the subconscious self-conversation goes. Unfortunately, this is largely spurred on by the unrealistic media and perpetuated by our sadly materialistic society.

I'm not trying to be a Debbie Downer and say that it's all bad to buy nice things. I have many nice things, and I know who I am and that I have nothing but good intentions and values deep down inside. So I do not judge anyone for what they purchase. I merely think it merits a conversation so that we can each discover why we make certain purchases and how they impact us personally.

At the end of the day, we all need to decide what our values are and what we feel best serves us individually. Would you feel better about yourself with an $800 purse on your arm or seeing that $800 in your bank account? Do you get more of a sense of self-worth from vanity or from security? Both can build self-confidence, so neither answer is right or wrong. What my experience tells me, from working with so many people and discussing finances with them over the years, is that the people who spent lots of money on luxury items were not much happier when their bank accounts were still weak. Because at night, when they logged in to see their bank statement, any self-esteem or confidence they had came right back down to earth under the stress of a lack of wealth. Money in the bank is better than spending on outward displays showing your success. Warren Buffett doesn't have much flash in his trappings — but he sure has the biggest flash in his confident smile! He is grounded and centered, and a great example for us all.

When in doubt, ask yourself, "Is this a *need* or a *want*?" If there is something you must spend money on because you absolutely need it, then so be it. But if the purchase is really a "want purchase," maybe you can set some business or earning goals and reward yourself with the purchase for hitting them. Let your wants drive you to be that much more disciplined and hard-working. Trust me, you will enjoy so much more what you worked tirelessly to acquire. And it's even more satisfying when it's attached to a milestone of achievement.

With e-commerce giants like Amazon making impulse buys easier than ever, U.S. online spending hit $1.2 trillion in 2025 — the "disposable income" illusion is stronger. But consider behavioral economics: Daniel Kahneman's research shows we regret impulse spending more than deliberate spending. To combat, use the "72-hour rule" — wait three days before buying non-essentials. Apps like PocketGuard categorize spending and highlight opportunity costs in real time. This not only saves money but trains your brain for delayed gratification, key to compounding wealth over decades.

Debt vs. Wealth

Thoughts are things, and we always attract more of what we focus on. Don't believe it? Take a look at hypochondriacs. These are well-meaning people who continually tell themselves that they are sick. They live in a perpetual state of moans and groans and constantly tell anyone who will listen about a new ache or pain they discover each day. It's easy to think that this is merely *psychological,* but there's a very real *physiological* result of their flawed mindset: Their brain actually sends signals to their organs telling them that they are indeed sick. As hard as it might be to believe, they've actually willed themselves into a sickened state.

The same brain functions are at play here. If you focus continually on *debt* (or even getting out of debt), you will tend to attract more of it. If you focus on *wealth,* you will attract wealth. Our goal throughout the book is to recalibrate your thinking to focus on building wealth. It works subtly, and over time, you are propelled in the direction of your thoughts.

If your goal all month long is to work hard to earn money in order to service your debts (pay bills), you'll forever be a slave to debt service. With debt on your mind, you will tend to attract more debt. But regardless of taking on more debt, let's consider your values. Your goal is to pay bills. So if you have $5,000 in bills, and you earn $6,000, you will pay the $5,000 to cover the bills and spend the leftover $1,000. The remaining thousand was a surplus — it was extra. So you reward yourself by going out to eat, taking a trip, buying new clothes, and finding other ways to spend it. Why not? After all, you've successfully met your goal of paying your bills, right?

Here's why this is a problem. Your focus could have been on *creating wealth* instead of servicing debt. It's a crucial shift in your mindset. It's a difference in your values. Do you need to spend money on today's things, or is becoming wealthy more important?

Here is a different way to think. Your goal all month long is to *grow your wealth*. You have $5,000 in bills, and you earn $6,000. The bills do get paid, but the remaining $1,000 is already earmarked for your wealth/investment account. You worked all month long to make enough money to have the extra that will increase your net worth. Always remember — a growing bank account will make you feel so much better about yourself than a fancy Rolex watch, expensive new shoes, or handbags.

What is more important to you?

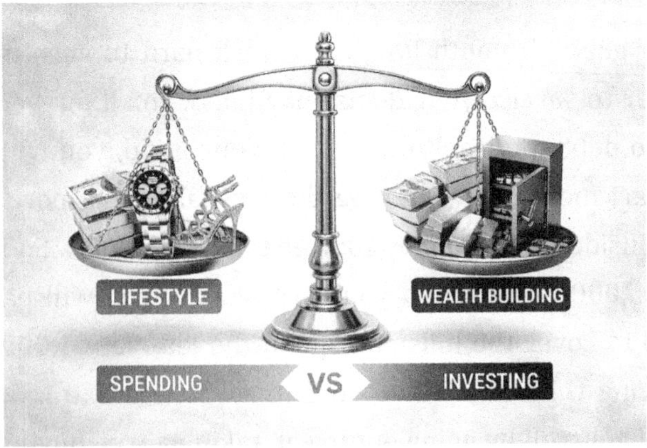

This is the crucial decision-making you must master. What are you working for? Debt or wealth? When you have the extra $1,000, where is it going? The choice is yours. And so are the consequences.

Modern neuroscience, via fMRI studies from UCLA, confirms "thoughts are things" — focusing on wealth activates brain regions linked to motivation and reward, boosting dopamine for action. With debt apps like Debt Payoff Planner visualizing progress, shift focus: Use vision boards or apps like Envision to picture wealth goals. This not only attracts opportunities but combats the $18.6 trillion U.S. debt crisis by prioritizing net worth over net bills.

Your Wealth Account

The very first thing you must do right now (if you have not done this already) is to open a new bank account that we will call your *Wealth Account.* This will be your doorway to a wealthy future. You want to be looking at this account balance monthly, or even weekly or daily. This account must always be growing! This is not your rainy-day fund for emergencies like a car repair, a hot water heater replacement, or a dental emergency. Those living expenses come out of your main working bank account, which you already have. This Wealth Account is not to be drained, but should be a one-way door for your money into your investment life. The only reason money comes out is if it is directed to a selected investment.

Remember, the goal is to take your focus off your debt and laser in on wealth creation. Set up your bills to be paid automatically from your checking account, so that you do not have to see them often. In your mind, you will now live in a world of abundance. You are leaving behind the world of lack or scarcity. Your head no longer occupies that space. You are now cutting unnecessary spending and growing your earnings to double the pace of your wealth's growth. It is exciting to mentally be living in this new realm!

You now have two income sources — one is your W-2 employee paycheck, or maybe your profits from a traditional business. Your second source is your business venture.

Here is one way to approach your finances with these two powerful economic engines. If you are building a part-time business venture while working a full-time job, then live off your W-2 income with the surplus (after bills) going to the Wealth Account. Then invest all of the proceeds from your business venture into your Wealth Account.

If you are already working full-time in your business venture as your sole source of income, you will need to determine how to service your debt while maintaining the priority of building your wealth. Again, the bills get paid, taxes put aside, and the rest you save/invest.

With high-yield online savings accounts offering rates up to 5 percent APY — far above traditional banks' 0.01 percent —

your Wealth Account can grow faster through compounding. Apps like Ally or Capital One 360 make setup seamless, with automatic transfers from paychecks. To enhance, link it to budgeting tools like YNAB for real-time tracking. This isn't just saving; it's strategic — consider FDIC-insured options for up to $250,000 protection, ensuring your "moat" against economic volatility.

Pay Yourself First

One of the most important wealth strategies you can employ is to pay yourself first. This means that before anyone you owe touches any of your incoming cash flow, you remember who is the number one priority. That's *you*, your family, and your future!

I learned from my mentor, Paul J Meyer, many years ago that before the money comes into your hand, you must already have a design for where it goes next. First, you have a set percentage right off the top that goes to you (your Wealth Account). In the beginning, this should be 10 percent. If you make $1,500/month, put away $150. If you make $3,000/month, put away $300. As your income grows, you grow this percentage because your cost of living should not increase at the same rate as your earnings growth.

For example, if you make $12,000/month, don't just stick to paying yourself $1,200. You don't need to elevate your cost of living to $10,800/month. You can easily live on $9,000 and put away $3,000, or live on $6,000 and invest $6,000. To see what this will do for your wealth accumulation, look at the chart at the top of the next page. It's similar to the previous accumulation chart, but this one shows the *repeated* efforts of your daily choices and how they compound over a variety of time spans.

Based on a 10% annual rate of return

	10 years	20 years	30 years	40 years
$5 day ($150/month)	$30,982	$114,854	$341,898	$956,517
$10 day ($300/month)	$61,965	$229,709	$683,797	$1,913,034
$20 day ($600/month)	$123,931	$459,418	$1,367,595	$3,826,068
$50 day ($3,500/month)	$309,828	$1,148,545	$3,418,987	$9,565,170
$100 day ($3,000/month)	$619,656	$2,297,090	$6,837,975	$19,130,340

It is vitally important that you make your wealth-building *automatic*. If you have to think about it every time you get paid, and have to consciously decide whether or not you want to pay yourself first and invest, you won't do it. You will keep putting it off. It is human nature. So you must *go to your boss right away* with urgency and ask that he/she take 10 percent of every paycheck and automatically transfer it into your new (separate) Wealth Account. Many employers can do this for you.

What if you are self-employed like me as a full-time entrepreneur? If your company cannot deduct the 10 percent before sending your commission checks to you, you can set up an automatic transfer with your bank to withdraw this 10 percent right out of your main checking or savings account. Many banks do this, so check around. By making this automatic, you eliminate the possibility that your *willpower* might fall short and that you'll decide to spend the money elsewhere.

Automation is easier than ever with fintech apps like Acorns or Qapital that round up purchases to invest in micro-amounts. For self-employed folks, tools like QuickBooks integrate with banks for seamless 10-20 percent transfers. Recent Vanguard studies show automated savers accumulate 3x more wealth over 10 years due to consistency. Start at 10 percent, but aim to scale to 15-20 percent as income grows — pair with Roth IRA contributions ($7,500 limit under 50) for tax-free growth, turning "pay yourself first" into a compounding powerhouse.

Give Some of it Away

Paul Meyer also insisted you carve a second 10 percent off the top to give away. Whether supporting a church or a charity, Paul taught me that all of what I have is God's by right of creation, and that I should do good things with some of what comes in. What he found in his life was that the more he gave, the more it came back tenfold (as long as he didn't give with

MINDSET NUGGETS

The wealthy don't panic; they prepare. Shift your mindset from reacting to anticipating.

the *expectation* of receiving). By becoming a giver, you will be living in a space of abundance and gratitude. In doing so, you will find that you will attract far more success into your life. And you will feel that the money that you are earning has far more meaning and impact. This also fends off the guilty feeling that can sometimes creep in when people start becoming wealthy. You might start questioning whether you deserve to live so much better than the rest of the world. By using some of your money to do good for others, you will instead feel driven and fulfilled.

So now we are at 20 percent off the top, leaving 80 percent to live on. I know what some may be thinking right about now. You're screaming out loud, "I can't even pay my bills with 100 percent of my current income, and you're telling me to take away 20 percent and make it happen with only the remaining 80 percent?" Let me ask you this. If bill collectors are already knocking on your door, do you think it's because you didn't have enough money, or because you didn't manage it properly? Many people are living paycheck to paycheck, and it's not always because they aren't earning enough — it's often because they haven't adopted the right habits. But here's the mindset shift: By committing to this 20 percent rule, you force yourself to get creative, cut unnecessary expenses, and perhaps even find ways to earn more. It's about prioritizing your future self.

So be disciplined about that 20 percent off the top. *Paying yourself first at least 10 percent of every dollar you earn is not an option*. Let me stop and say this as boldly as I can: *If you will not do this, you will never get wealthy.*

Giving is more impactful through platforms like GoFundMe or donor-advised funds via Fidelity, which allow tax deductions of up to 60 percent of AGI for cash gifts. Research from Giving USA shows U.S. charitable giving hit $557 billion in 2025, with givers reporting higher life satisfaction. Start small: Automate 5-10 percent to causes via apps like RoundUp, where purchases round up for charity. This not only builds karma but qualifies for itemized deductions, reducing taxable income — turning generosity into a smart financial strategy for abundance.

Biblical Stewardship: Managing Money as a Faithful Servant

This section might make some of you uncomfortable. That's not my intent. I realize that people have different belief systems, a variety of faiths, and even no faith at all. I respect all the above. At the same time, I identify as a Christian, and because it drives how I live my life in every regard, it would be irresponsible for me to pretend like my faith didn't drive my finances. For this reason, I want to share my thoughts on how the Bible views money and the stewardship of it. Even if you don't subscribe to my convictions, read this section with an open mind because I believe its principles are largely universal regardless of which side of the spiritual spectrum you're on.

Money is a tool, a resource, not a *source*. God is the Source; money is what He entrusts to us to manage wisely. Too many people treat wealth as the ultimate goal, attaching their identity, security, and significance to it. But Scripture is clear: Deuteronomy 8:18 says, "You shall remember the Lord your God, for it is He who gives you the power to get wealth." That power — wisdom, opportunity, multiplication — comes from Him. He wouldn't highlight wealth unless there was virtue in it. The key is stewardship: using what He gives to glorify Him and bless others.

The Parable of the Talents (Matthew 25:14–30) drives this home. A master entrusts his servants with money — five talents (as the currency was known back then), two talents, and one talent — each according to their ability. The first two invest and double their portions; the third buries his in fear. The master rewards the faithful servants with more responsibility and joy, but condemns the fearful one as "wicked and slothful." The lesson is simple: we are stewards of what God gives us — time, talents, treasure. Burying it is not humility; it's disobedience. We're called to multiply, not hoard. Whether it's growing a business, investing wisely, or sharing resources, the expectation is faithful management and growth.

This ties directly to generosity. 2 Corinthians 9:6–11 reminds us: "Whoever sows sparingly will also reap sparingly, and whoever sows bountifully will also reap bountifully. Each one must give as he has decided in his heart, not reluctantly or under compulsion, for God loves a cheerful giver." God doesn't want duty-bound giving; He wants joyful, willing hearts. When we give generously — whether tithing, supporting causes, or blessing others — He promises to supply and multiply our seed, enriching us so we can be generous in every way. Generosity isn't loss; it's *overflow*. It produces thanksgiving to God and glorifies Him through our actions.

The Rich Young Ruler (Matthew 19:16–30) illustrates the danger of misplaced trust. He kept the commandments but clung to his possessions. When Jesus told him to sell everything and follow, he walked away sorrowful. Jesus then said it's hard for a rich man to enter the kingdom, even using a hyperbolic illustration showing that it would be easier for a camel to go through the eye of a needle! The disciples were stunned: "Who then can be saved?" Jesus answered, "With man this is impossible, but with God all things are possible." The point isn't that wealth is evil; it's that it can become an idol. When money masters you instead of you mastering it, it blocks surrender to God. But when God is your source, wealth becomes a tool for greater good. When Peter asked what they'd gain for leaving everything, Jesus promised a hundredfold in this life and eternal life beyond.

Here's the bottom line: money amplifies who you already are. If your heart is on possessions, wealth will expose it. If your heart is on God and others, wealth becomes a force for good. I've seen both sides — people who hoard and feel empty, and people who give generously and experience joy and multiplication. Paul J. Meyer, my mentor and a billionaire, gave away over $400 million while alive, and his foundation continues that work. He taught me: the more you give without expecting return, the more comes back — often in unexpected ways.

With household debt at a current $18.6 trillion and economic uncertainty, stewardship matters more than ever. I always advise people to start small: tithe cheerfully, give to causes that move you, and track how giving shifts your mindset from scarcity to abundance. Teach your family: money is a gift to steward, not own. When you manage it faithfully, God multiplies it — not just for you, but for His purposes. Decide on a giving goal (e.g., 10% of income or a specific cause). Set up an automatic transfer to a charity or church. Track how it feels — notice the shift from fear to joy. Remember: stewardship isn't about perfection; it's about faithfulness. God entrusts us with more as we prove trustworthy with little.

Building Resilience in Uncertain Times

As we give some of our wealth away, it's crucial to remember that true financial freedom isn't just about accumulation — it's about endurance. In today's world, with modest inflation lingering above 2 percent, a cooling job market, and potential economic shifts on the horizon, building resilience is key to protecting what you've earned.

I've seen too many people build wealth only to watch it erode because they weren't prepared for the unexpected. Think about it: Inflation might not be skyrocketing like in recent years, but even a steady 2-3 percent rise means your money buys less over time. A resilient mindset means viewing these challenges not as threats but as opportunities to strengthen your foundation. Start by creating an emergency fund that covers 6-12 months of expenses — put it in a high-yield savings account earning around 4-5 percent in 2026 rates. This isn't just savings; it's peace of mind.

Embrace scenario planning: Ask yourself, "What if my income dips by 20 percent?" or "How would higher interest rates affect my plans?" This isn't fear-mongering; it's empowerment. I learned this from my mentors — always have a Plan B. Diversify your skills, just as you diversify your investments. In a gig economy where side hustles are booming, upskilling through online courses can open new doors. Remember, resilience is a muscle. Exercise it by staying informed — track economic indicators like unemployment rates (projected to hover around 4.5 percent in 2026) and adjust accordingly.

The wealthy don't panic; they prepare. Shift your mindset from reacting to anticipating. When uncertainty hits, you'll not only survive but thrive, turning potential setbacks into stepping stones toward greater wealth.

Post-pandemic lessons show resilient portfolios weathered 2022's 18 percent market drop better, with 20-30 percent in cash equivalents. Apps like YNAB simulate scenarios; pair with mental health tools like Calm for stress reduction — APA links financial worry to 25 percent higher anxiety, which is a mindset killer.

Understanding Inflation and Protecting Your Wealth

Inflation erodes purchasing power — think of it as a silent tax on your savings. As of early 2026, U.S. inflation is around 2.7 percent, with forecasts for 2.4–2.7 percent throughout the year. Even at low levels, it adds up: $100 today might buy only $78 in 20 years at 2.5 percent inflation.

The resilient mindset? Protect your wealth by diversifying into inflation hedges. TIPS (Treasury Inflation-Protected Securities) adjust principal with CPI. Commodities such as gold and real estate often rise with inflation. Stocks in sectors like energy or consumer staples can outpace it in the long term.

MINDSET NUGGETS

Pay yourself first and build your Wealth Account.

Constantly reduce your debt to others.

Track it: Monitor CPI reports and adjust your budget — aim for investments returning 4–7 percent above inflation. This isn't fear; it's foresight. My mentors taught me: Wealth isn't just earning; it's preserving.

Debt Free is the New Lamborghini

Do you want to wield the ultimate status symbol? Get debt-free. Seriously. Being debt-free is the most desirable financial achievement in the world today. Entire nations are imploding under the weight of their financial distress. Companies are shuttering their doors forever. (Remember Blockbuster Video? Montgomery Ward's? Compaq? Sears?) Personal bankruptcies are at an all-time high. American consumers alone owe a staggering $18.6 trillion in debt (as of this writing), and our students owe a crippling $1.8 trillion in student loan debt. The burden of this debt is not only financially devastating but also psychologically paralyzing, with rising delinquencies signaling that many are struggling to keep up.

Wouldn't it feel amazing to be debt-free? I bet you would feel liberated to owe nobody. The weight of debt on people's shoulders is one of the main causes of stress and a leading cause of marital arguments. When people say money isn't important, I don't get it. If it's not important, why does it cause so much strife? One of my goals for building wealth is to help people get on the other side of money. I don't want to teach people just how to make money, but rather how never to be a slave to it again. I want people to rid themselves of the stress that comes from debt and to live happier, more fulfilled lives.

For many, the dream of being debt-free is just that — a dream. Of course, everyone would love the joy of not owing anything to anyone. But why do so few ever get completely out of debt? The reason is that most people have no plan. You have to have a plan to get there. What has your plan been thus far? Was it just hoping that the debt would just disappear over time? I find that the people who don't have a plan to get out of debt usually end up with more debt over time. It's like drifting on a boat without a rudder — you'll end up wherever the currents take you, which is rarely where you want to go.

When you borrow money to pay for something, you must consider how much the interest charges will be to determine the actual price you will end up paying for that purchase. For example, if you buy a car for $30,000 with an interest rate of 7 percent over a five-year loan, add $5,600 interest to the principal purchase price. So you really end up paying $35,600, not $30,000. If you buy a computer for $800 on your credit card and assume you are not paying off the full credit balance each month, you are really paying much more for that computer. Let's assume your card's interest rate is 24 percent, and that you finally pay the computer off in three years. Add $324 in interest charges to the initial price tag, bringing the actual cost to $1,124! This is why I don't believe in buying on credit cards unless you pay it off in full at the end of the month to avoid these interest charges.

Is all debt created equal? There may be good debt and bad debt. Let me attack credit cards first. I use credit cards for payment convenience, and my bank account automatically pays them off each month. Therefore, I never pay interest on this money. And I get reward points on those purchases. But for most people, credit card debt is bad.

You spent money that you did not have, assuming you are not paying off the balance every month. Spending money that you don't have on purchases that are not intended to make you money is sending you in the opposite direction of growing wealth or becoming debt-free. We will cover this topic shortly when we discuss creating a personal budget. Credit card debt is usually the most expensive, often charging 24 percent or more in interest. Your goal may always have been to pay the minimum payment each month, but this is what the bank wants you to do. Understand one thing — the banks do not want you to ever pay off your credit card balance. When you do, they stop earning money from you! They want you to keep rolling your balance forward each month, making only your minimum payment to keep you in good standing.

My goal for you is to pay down this balance with everything you can, as fast as you can. I use credit cards because they are a convenient (and safer than debit cards) way to pay for things. But I urge you to use credit cards only if you will do the same. Otherwise, the interest charges erode the wealth you are attempting to accumulate.

Let's remember, part of your plan is to pay yourself first and build your Wealth Account. Alongside this investing/saving strategy, you must also constantly reduce your debt to others. This part requires us to use some common sense. What debt should you pay off first? Start out by taking all of your bills and lining them up across your kitchen table. Arrange them in the order of highest interest rate to lowest. The rule of thumb that often makes the most sense is to pay off the highest-rate debt first, as it is costing you the most money to carry. This is usually your credit card debt. Then you might have student loans, and then at the bottom is likely the mortgage on your home. This is often referred to as the Avalanche Method. (You should check your mortgage interest rate against the prevailing market rates today. If your rate is 1 ½ percent higher than the market, it may make sense to refinance this debt to lower your rate and payment.)

You can also use the Snowball Method: List your debts from smallest to largest, pay minimums on all but the smallest, and throw everything extra at that one until it's gone. Then roll that payment into the next. This builds momentum. Whichever method you choose, track progress monthly. Celebrate small wins to stay motivated.

Psychological studies from APA link debt to 20 percent higher depression rates — freedom reduces this. And remember, being debt-free isn't just about numbers — it's a mindset. Once you're free, you'll view money as a tool for growth, not a chain holding you back.

With buy-now-pay-later services like Affirm or Klarna mimicking credit cards but often with hidden fees up to 30 percent, "bad debt" traps are more insidious. A 2025 CFPB report shows 43 percent of BNPL users face delinquencies, exacerbating stress, linked to 25 percent higher anxiety per APA studies. Use apps like Debt Payoff Planner to simulate scenarios: e.g., paying $200 extra monthly on a 24 percent card shaves years off and saves thousands. Mindset: View debt as leverage only if ROI exceeds cost — otherwise, it's a wealth killer. Pair with credit monitoring tools like Credit Karma for proactive management, turning debt from a burden to a strategic tool.

Good Debt vs. Bad Debt

Is there really such a thing as "good debt?" Let's peg the average return on your investments at 10 percent. Any debt that costs you less than 10 percent is not really bad debt as you crunch the numbers. This is true as long as your money is being directed into investments that truly earn you more than what you are paying to service debt. The first goal is to pay off all debts that exceed your investment returns.

For most people, the ultimate goal is to be flat-out debt-free. In simplest terms, that should be your goal, too. But at some point, you might become a more savvy investor. You may calculate that you can increase your wealth by carrying some debt. For example, if your mortgage rate is only 4 percent, and you can get a 10 percent return by investing, it makes sense to carry a mortgage because your net effect is 6 percent positive. On top of that, the government in some countries, like the U.S., allows you to write off the interest on your mortgage. (As of this writing, for mortgages originated after December 15, 2017, the limit for deductible interest is $750,000 — $375,000 if married filing separately). For mortgages incurred before that date, the grandfathered limit is $1 million ($500,000 if married filing separately). So in essence, the government is paying for part of your house payment. As much as I like the idea of being debt-free, I also like making money. So I personally carry the maximum mortgage on my home, thus borrowing at 4 percent so that I can get a much higher return on my own cash and pocket the difference.

For those of you in the early stages of teaching yourselves about money, I suggest keeping it simple and making it your priority to go *Debt-Free ASAP*. That ought to be your mantra. Some will put the words on their dream boards. Some will write the words on their bathroom mirrors. I am not totally opposed to this. But remember that we get more of what we focus on. So even though we are saying we want to get rid of debt, we are still talking about debt. If you are motivated by a war or attack on something bad, then that's fine. But I would rather you keep your focus on the positive, and write on your mirror or dream board — BUILD WEALTH or BUILD NET WORTH. The reason is that being debt-free merely brings you to ground zero. You are not wealthy just because you are out of debt. You are out of the negative. The danger is in setting our goals too low. If you set a goal and hit it but are still not happy, you set it too low in the first place. Your expectations of what life would be like after achieving that goal will let you down.

With average credit card rates at 24 percent vs. stock market returns averaging 10 percent, "bad debt" like cards (no asset backing) drains wealth — pay off first. "Good debt" examples: Student loans at 5-7 percent for career-boosting education, or mortgages at 5.9 percent building equity. But with $1.8 trillion student debt burdens, vet "good" debt: Calculate ROI — e.g., a degree boosting salary by $20K/year justifies 6 percent loans. Use calculators like Bankrate's to compare. The mindset here is that debt is a tool, not a trap — leverage it wisely for net positive gains.

Proclaim Your Goals

I am glad we are on the topic of goals. There's an old saying that *if you don't know where you want to go, any road will take you there*. Goals set us in motion and prompt us to chase something each day with a sense of purpose. I simply cannot imagine living a life without goals, wandering aimlessly through the days. The key to goals is that you must dig deep and find goals that motivate you — move you to act. Your goals can include others, but they essentially are yours.

I believe that goals must be:

- specific
- written
- attached to a deadline
- worthwhile
- shared with others.

Many people have goals for the income they want to earn per month/year. But we need to go to the next level and have goals for that money you are earning. So set a goal to create wealth. Define it.

- How much money will you have invested?
- How much cash in the bank?
- How much will your investment income be per year?
- When will you achieve this?
- What will change in your life when this goal is met?

Along the way, just one of the steps to achieving your wealth goals will be to become debt-free. Just remember, this is an important milestone, but not your end game! Debt-free means you owe nothing to anybody ... but it could be possible that you don't have much wealth either. So focus on setting these goals, share them with your family so they understand the importance, and then go figure out how you will make it happen.

Let's stop right now and help you discover goals that ignite your fire, and let's write these goals down in the form of a proclamation.

I am officially **debt-free** on this date:

____

I feel liberated.

I have true freedom.

I am planning a celebration trip to:

____

I will reward myself with:

____

I am officially **wealthy** on this date:

____

I have this much net worth on this date:

____

I feel secure.

I have peace of mind.

My investments generate an annual cash flow of:

____

MINDSET NUGGETS

Download FREE printable Wealth and Debt-Free Proclamations at *mindsettomillionsbook.com/free*

So you now have put your mind to work on creating *specific* goals that move you. You have *written* them down. You attached *deadlines* to them. You decided these are *worthwhile* goals. And you can now share them with people in your life. An essential part of turning goals into reality is speaking them into your mindset every day. Reinforcing positive thoughts will burn the belief into your soul that you are accomplishing your goals. So here is a possible Daily Affirmation you can read aloud to yourself every morning and every night:

DAILY WEALTH AFFIRMATION

I am focused every day on building my wealth. I love building wealth for all the good I will use it for. My financial freedom allows me to call my own shots, live life on my own terms, and I am excited about today. I am enjoying the wealth-building journey because I know that what I learn and grow through will be just as valuable as the empire I am building. I am smart with my money, and I am a great financial role model. I do not spend money frivolously. Every dollar I save, I can invest. Every dollar I invest increases my empire. As my empire grows, so does my ability to influence

> *others and to be a resource supporting great causes and helping others. I have the Wealth Mindset, and I am attracting wealth every day, including today.*

Put this affirmation in front of you for easy access every day. Go onto our website to print a gorgeous copy for yourself.

You can use goal-setting apps like GoalsOnTrack or Habitica to gamify proclamations, along with AI reminders and progress tracking. Harvard Business Review studies show shared goals are 65 percent more likely to be achieved — post on social or accountability groups. Use the goal-setting tips I mentioned earlier; e.g., "Invest $50K in index funds by Dec 2027, yielding $5K annual passive income." This turns proclamations into actionable plans, accelerating wealth amid economic uncertainties.

Buy In

It is critically important that you contemplate how these goals and your new mindset will impact those around you. If you are married or have children, this might instigate a change in lifestyle. Where you used to spend freely, take them places and buy them things ... suddenly you have become this money monster. You have cut off the money tree, and they aren't going to like it one bit. This is why you must get their buy-in on this new vision and game plan. They must see *why* you want to make these changes, and most importantly, show them what's in it for them. If they do not feel the same way about your mission to cut spending and use excess revenues to invest in the future, you will have one unhappy situation.

Your value system may be changing. But theirs is still the same as it was yesterday. So you will need to work on convincing them to get on the same page as you. How? You will sell them on the *vision* of your future dream lifestyle, one enveloped in wealth, security, and freedom. In essence, you will have to recruit them onto your team. It will take everyone operating as a team — *for* the team. They will need to find their own ways to cut spending habits. They will need to support the frugality going forward, rather than undermine your efforts. If they have bought into the grand *vision* of becoming debt-free, financially independent, and wealthy, you will move more easily towards your goals.

Another way to get your family on the same page with you is to read this book together. Study it and use it to help create your plan. Some family members might have a W-2 mindset and might not have the same entrepreneurial blood running through their veins. Inch them toward your world by watching entrepreneurial shows on TV, reading the right books, and even sharing stories of people who have made it. Help them envision their dream lifestyle, then show them stories of how people have achieved it through the same business model as yours and by developing a wealth-building mindset. Help them to see themselves as *unbroke*.

Using jars as a living metaphor can make it real. There are fun ways — especially with children — to get their buy-in. For example, many parents I've mentored in entrepreneurship have used the children's desire to take a trip to Disney World. So they had their kids cut out pictures of Mickey Mouse, the Princess, or their favorite characters. They got a huge plastic jar and glued the pictures to the side. They told the kids that whenever mom or dad went to a business meeting, they would each get 50 cents to put into the jar. Once the jar is filled, they will use this money to take the family to Disney World. You wouldn't believe how excited the kids got. They would ask, "Mom, why aren't you going to a meeting tonight?" How's that for a reversal? That's true buy-in. What if you did that for the wealth-building plan buy-in as well? Find ways for the household to contribute to the wealth jar, and once it fills up and is deposited into the bank, the family gets to do something amazing.

With family finances strained by rising costs — average household expenses up 20 percent since 2020 — buy-in is crucial for unity. Use apps like Honeydue for shared budgeting, where everyone logs spending and sees progress toward goals. Psychological research from the Gottman Institute shows financial alignment reduces marital conflict by 30 percent.

Host family "wealth nights" with games like Monopoly or apps like Wealthfront's simulators to make it fun, teaching kids fiscal responsibility early — turning potential resistance into collaborative excitement for abundance.

How to Keep the Money You Make

It's not how much you make, it's how much you keep that matters most. This section primarily pertains to entrepreneurs running home-based businesses, since I believe that's the best economic model out there, bar none. For a 1099 independent business owner, you get tax advantages that employees do not. The typical home-based business owner can legitimately save anywhere from $2,000-$5,000 a year (or much more) of in-pocket tax savings just by operating a small business in pursuit of making a profit — even if they don't actually turn a profit! Just starting a business venture is not enough. You must be pursuing profits by doing money-making activities. Be prudent about documenting your activities so that if you are ever questioned, you can emphatically demonstrate that you had the intent to make a profit. As long as you can prove this, you will have the ability to write off many expenditures as business expenses. In other words, you deduct those expenses from your income total *before* paying taxes on the lowered amount.

Do you need income that exceeds your expenses to write them off? Actually, no, you don't. To the extent that you spent more than you earned, the excess expense can be carried over and applied against your income in future years. This is called a business loss carry-forward. Your business loss can even be deducted from the ordinary income from your job. This is often the case, as new business owners may spend more than they earn from the new business in the beginning. This does not mean your business is not working. It just means businesses take time to build and become profitable, and the government understands this. So if you lost/spent more than you earned for the first couple of years in your business venture (which is common in any business start-up), it comes back to you in a way. You will carry that loss forward and deduct it in the first profitable year. So keep investing and planting seeds to build your business.

Just so you can appreciate the tax benefits of building a business like this, let's briefly touch on the difference between you and a person who gets paid as a W-2 employee. As an employee, you get a salary, the government subtracts its taxes from the full amount, and then you get what's left over. But as a 1099 business owner, you earn your commissions, you deduct your business expenses, and then pay taxes based *on that lower amount.*

Here is a rudimentary example:

Job Salary — $50,000

Taxable Income — $50,000

Government taxes at 20 percent — $10,000 taxes paid

Business Venture Income — $50,000

Subtract Write-offs/Deductions — Minus $10,000

Taxable Income — $40,000

Taxes at 20 percent — $8,000 taxes paid

The great thing about running a business out of your home is that you get to write off any expenses that are connected to your pursuit of a profit. Here are some examples (get specific details from a tax expert/CPA):

Home office expense — If 20 percent of the square footage of your home is used for business (office, supplies storage, etc.), you get to write off that percentage of your mortgage/rent payment, of the utilities, and of house cleaning

Car expense — You can write off actual costs for your car, gas, maintenance, and washes, or you can write off a set amount per mile you drove the car for business purposes. As of this writing, the rate is 72.5 cents per business-driven mile! Be sure to keep a daily log of the business miles. So if you drove

20 miles to drive to a business appointment, you write off $14.50. The government, in essence, just paid for a few gallons of your gas!

Meals — Any time you meet with prospects for a bite or conduct a team meeting at a restaurant, you get to write off a percentage of your check.

Travel/Hotels — Any travel that is business-related (meaning you did business as the reason for the trip), you can write off your plane ticket and lodging. You are allowed to take in the scenery and enjoy yourself, too.

Here are other categories that may be eligible for write-off.

Tools/Supplies/Printing

Website design/hosting

Telecommunications

Event tickets for briefings, trainings, conventions

Awards/Contest prizes

Contributions to Retirement Plans

Office Furniture

You can even hire your spouse or kids, which will entitle you to tax advantages as well. For example, if you hire your spouse, you can write off your medical expenses! Otherwise, this is not normally a tax write-off.

Be sure to keep all receipts and records. Even if it is a toll in your car for $3, every dollar adds up. Track *everything*. There are many ways to do this. Some people are old-fashioned, throwing every paper receipt in a file box and sorting it out at the end of the year. Others are more modern and use tax software, making expense entries each night to stay totally on top of it.

One tip I use is to always use one business credit card or checking account for all business use. This way, everything is always tracked by simply pulling my account statement. Of course, you will have your box of paper receipts to journal every expense, should you ever get an audit letter. There are now apps that allow you to do that on your mobile device by simply snapping a photo of the receipt.

In addition to tracking your expenditures, keep a physical calendar of your activities. This might be needed to prove that you are actually pursuing the business in the early days when your profits are lower than your expenses. Keep a log of the training calls you listen to, the events you attend, the appointments you conduct, and the prospecting activities you do. Order updated company materials, tools, and products regularly. Basically, do what you would expect to do to build your business. Just track and document it.

With IRS audits up 15 percent due to AI-flagged discrepancies, tracking is non-negotiable. Apps like Expensify or QuickBooks Self-Employed auto-categorize via photo scans and integrate with banks for seamless 1099 reporting. For home-based businesses, the simplified home office deduction is $5/sq ft (up to 300 sq ft, max $1,500), but itemized methods yield more for larger spaces. Expand deductions: Virtual meetings via Zoom count as telecom; online ads as marketing. Mindset: View taxes as a partnership — maximizing deductions isn't evasion; it's smart stewardship, freeing capital for reinvestment.

Paying Your Taxes

Please note that this section is written from my perspective as an American. Readers in other countries would do well to heed their respective governments' tax laws.

We talked about the benefits of home business tax deductions. Tax codes and rules change often, so be sure to consult with an expert tax accountant. The next key to wealth building is to treat taxes seriously. Pay what you owe, and *pay on time.*

Our taxes pay for the police, fire department, schools, roads, military, and the freedoms we all enjoy. As often as I think that our tax rates are far too high, I pay them with pride. I once had a goal to earn six figures in a year. Then I had a goal to pay six figures in taxes in a year. Now I pay multiple six-figure tax bills. I feel lucky to have been blessed enough to earn this money, so I pay my share to help keep the system going for us all. I see many people trying to cheat the system and avoid paying taxes. Let me warn you, it will always catch up with you. Most of the time, the government will track you down ... and if they don't, karma will! Just live by the rule of doing what's right when no one is looking. That's what it means to have character.

Paying *on time* is critical. First of all, if you are late in paying, you tack on fines and penalties. This costs you even more than your fair share and wastes money that you could have invested. This is often caused by not being diligent about paying as the money comes in and not setting aside your estimated taxes as you go along. If you estimate that you will be in a 20 percent tax bracket, then put aside 20 percent of every check you get for taxes. Put this into a separate account from your spending account. Do not touch this money under any circumstances!

Once you get through your first year and have established a record of earnings, you will be expected to pay "quarterly estimated taxes" from then on. In other words, you will need to estimate what your earnings will be for the calendar year, deduct your estimated expenses, multiply the net amount by your tax rate, and pay one-fourth of that every quarter. If at year-end you did not earn quite that much and you overpaid, or you underestimated your business expenses, you will request a refund when you file your tax return that spring.

I have witnessed many entrepreneurs fall short on paying taxes. They let it get away from them, and the next thing they know, they owe the government many thousands of dollars more than they possess. The last person you want to owe money to is the government. They can garnish your income and even seize your assets. Be smart; be disciplined. As I have said before, "You must have self-discipline, or the world will discipline you. Either way, you will get disciplined."

Set a Personal Budget

You have to inspect what you expect. Budgeting is planning your cash flow. How much will you have coming in, and how much will be going out? If you don't track it, you cannot control it. This is a common problem for people who struggle financially. If I ask them to show me their budget, they look back at me, confused. Budgeting was never taught in high school, and not taught in general college studies. Most parents don't have a budget, so they surely have not taught this to their kids. The good news is that if you decide to act on the principles of this book and create a budget, you will be far ahead of the crowd.

Readers of this book can download a free sample personal budget. (See Mindset Nuggets.) Once downloaded, you will see that you are expected to set a goal for spending in each category, then, at month-end, write in your actual amount spent. This will give you the ability to review where you are overspending, and help you to establish your goals for next month to improve. Seeing your spending habits on paper will give you a clear picture of your financial situation. You will be able to see which expenses are truly necessary and cannot be reduced, and which might have some flexibility. Of course, you always want to raise your top-line income. But to build wealth faster, look for ways to cut down on personal spending at the same time.

MINDSET NUGGETS

Download a FREE Monthly personal budget at

mindsettomillionsbook.com/free

Set a Business Budget

Just like your life needs a personal budget to plan and track your income and your living expenses, so does your business. Your business will require an investment to get started and grow. There are costs for lead generation, websites, materials, cell phones, transportation, etc. Some might think the more you spend, the more you will make. This is not always true, but generally it has some merit. The key to your business budget is to be thoughtful in your planning and in your review. I initially set a goal of spending $300 in a month to generate some prospects. If I found that after the campaign, it returned $500 to me, I would scale it up the next month to double the spend. If that $600 yielded a proportionate return, I could decide to continue moving the campaign forward. But if I budgeted money for a project and it did not yield results, I would review the plan and make changes accordingly.

Money does not come from thin air. Nobody has an unlimited budget for spending. Knowing this, it is imperative that you decide how much total money you can invest each month in your business. Then you can allocate portions of that total to the various activities or needs of your business. Remember, you have to see your cash flow in order to make the best decisions. Therefore, getting your budget on paper is very important.

The Power of Side Hustles: Diversifying Your Income Streams

You've set your budgets — personal and business. Now, let's talk about accelerating your wealth by not putting all your eggs in one basket. In 2026, with economic resilience top of mind, the power of side hustles has never been greater. I fell in love with entrepreneurship because it taught me that one income stream is risky; multiple streams create a river of abundance.

Think about it: Relying solely on a job or a single business is like driving with no spare tire. Side hustles — whether freelancing, online sales, or gig work — can add 20-50 percent to your income without quitting your main gig. I've mentored people who started with simple ideas, like turning a hobby into an Etsy shop or driving for rideshare services, and watched their wealth grow exponentially. I believe so strongly in the power of the side hustle that I wrote an entire book about it, called *Untrapped Freedom Manifesto: Become an Entrepreneur to Escape the Grind and Find Freedom & Happiness.*

The mindset here? Opportunity is everywhere. In today's digital world, platforms make it easy to monetize skills — coding, writing, or even pet-sitting. Gig platforms like Upwork or Fiverr reported $4.7 billion in U.S. earnings, per Upwork data — the average hustler adds $5K/year. I've also built a fortune in the network marketing space, where six- and seven-figure incomes are being built on a daily basis, and I've personally witnessed thousands of regular people earn extraordinary incomes on the side. Because of my vast experience in this "side-business space," I have to emphasize that it is way smarter to start your own side business than to get a second job as a side hustle, trading your time for dollars. You already trade your time for money at your 9-5 job, so from 5-9, you should be building *your* fortune/enterprise.

But it's not just about extra cash; it's about building a resilient mindset. Start small: Dedicate 5-10 hours a week. Track earnings like business expenses, and funnel 50 percent straight to your wealth account. Watch out for burnout — balance is key. Remember, the wealthy have an average of seven income streams. Why? Because when one dips (like in a job market cooling to 4-5 percent unemployment), others flow stronger.

Adopt this: "I'm not just an employee; I'm an income architect." It shifts you from scarcity to abundance. My early side ventures compounded my main business success. Yours can too. Slow down to assess opportunities, then speed up with action. This is how empires are fortified.

THE INVESTING MINDSET

How to Invest Your Money

So you've earned some money. You have deducted your expenses and paid taxes on the taxable portion. Now, what's the next step towards growing this net income and becoming wealthy? It's no small step that you've gotten here! Whether you have a surplus of $50 a month to invest, or $500, or $5,000, the plan will be much the same. There are many ways to invest your money and put it to work for you. As I have also heard it, "Send your money out into the world and have it come back with friends!"

I have found that you can rank investment ideas by return and importance. You also must ask whether you want to invest your money to grow your current business or to invest in something completely separate. Here are my investment areas:

1. Back into your business

2. Into yourself

3. Stocks

4. Bonds

5. Money Market / CDs

6. Real estate

7. Life Insurance

8. Other Businesses

9. Tax-deferred plans

Let's explore each of these investment options.

Investing Back into Your Business

I had a mentor who once told me that the best investment I could make, better than any stock pick, would be to invest back into my business ventures. My business is your/my cash machine. If you can pump money back into the machine to make it turn out even bigger profits, what could be better? So this is what I did. I looked for every way that I could employ my money to grow my machine. Here are some things I invested money into for my particular business (yours may look different depending on the type of business you might have):

- Tools — videos, brochures, websites, etc.
- Lead generation
- Hosting luncheons and dinners
- Running team contests and incentives
- Personal development for my team

Digital tools like Canva for brochures or Leadpages for websites costing $10-50/month make reinvestment more efficient. Track ROI via Google Analytics or a CRM like HubSpot (free tier). Example: $500 on Facebook ads yielding 50 leads, converting 10 percent to $5K revenue, can yield a 10X return. Amid the gig economy, invest in upskilling via Coursera ($49/course). Mindset: Business as compounding asset — reinvest 10-20 percent of your profits monthly for exponential growth, turning ventures into self-sustaining empires.)

Investing in Yourself

It can be argued that investing in yourself should rank above investing in your business. But I will rank this at number two, only because it is not as immediate or as easy to measure. As

I stated earlier, in order for your income to grow, you need to grow. If you ever want to earn six figures, or even seven figures a year, you need to become the person who deserves such an income. You must grow your mind, attitude, skills, and personality.

Here are some ways that I have invested in myself over the years:

- Books
- CDs/audios
- Attending seminars
- Training events
- All of the above for people on my team

In your line of work, this list will likely look different, but hopefully, you get the idea. The greatest investment you can make is in yourself and your own development.

In the grand scheme of things, this area does not require a particularly large financial investment. It is mostly time investment, in reading books and listening to audios. Once in a while, you might spend $500 to attend a workshop on a certain skill you want to develop. This cost might reach $1,500 when you factor in a plane ticket, a hotel room, and meals. It pains me to hear people say they cannot afford to make such investments or that it is simply not worth their time. These people are sadly mistaken and are, frankly, uncoachable. And for this reason, I predict they will fail.

Author and speaker Charlie "Tremendous" Jones always taught, "You will be the same person five years from now that you are today, except for the people you meet and the books you read." We need to get around people who could have a positive influence on us. These monthly events and workshops help us create an environment that promotes growth and success. And this gets us around people who can help us succeed. We must stop hanging around with people who have the same problems and get around those who have the solutions.

When I learned of a great book or audio, I would buy hundreds of them to get into my team's hands. A follower will read a book and say, "That was a great book," and then put it aside. A leader says, "This is a good book, I need to get my entire team reading it!" That leader promotes it day and night, and uses it as a tool to train and develop his/her people. So invest in developing yourself and your people.

Self-investment is digital: Audiobooks via Audible ($15/month), seminars on MasterClass ($10/month), or free TED Talks. ROI? A Harvard study shows continuous learners earn 20 percent more. Team-wide: Platforms like LinkedIn Learning ($30/user/month) for shared courses. Mindset: You're your best asset — allocate 5 percent of your income monthly to growth, like AI skills via Coursera, boosting employability amid 4.4 percent unemployment for long-term wealth.

Investing in Stocks

One great thing about investing in the stock market is that the market provides liquidity. It is very simple to buy stocks online these days in just a few seconds. And it is just as easy to go online and sell stock if you want to liquidate or raise some cash.

What you should do first is decide what kind of investor you want to be — passive or active. Do you want to invest in a fund and let the professional fund managers pick the stocks and manage your account for you, or do you want to take on the job of picking, buying, and managing this yourself? If you are brand new to investing, I suggest you go with a fund. This way, your money can be invested and grow without you losing focus or having to become a stock and financial planning expert.

There are mutual funds and index funds. A mutual fund is simply a grouping of stocks picked by the fund manager. A typical mutual fund may hold 100 stocks. This gives you diversification across many companies, which reduces your risk of a few companies doing poorly and losing much of your investment. These funds can be found grouped in many ways.

You can buy a fund focused on companies in technology, energy, transportation, real estate, industrials, or other sectors. This gives you exposure to multiple stocks in a single investment vehicle. The premise of investing in a particular mutual fund is that the fund manager you select might be a better stock picker than other managers, and thus outperform the rest in the market. So investors often research mutual fund managers' track records over the last several years to find those in their groove, investing in the right places.

Mutual funds should be bought with some understanding of how they function. You are giving your money to the manager to buy the stocks he has chosen for the fund. During the time you own this fund, you will likely see the manager sell some of the stocks and replace them with others that he feels are better investments at that time. You will pay fees to the fund managers for their expertise, services, and transaction processing. At the time of this writing, the average mutual fund fees are about 0.40 percent of the value of your investment each year. While this is not a high percentage, you need to ask and know the precise fees you will be charged. Even fractional percentages can chip away at your long-term wealth accumulation. A half percent compounded over years could mean the difference of hundreds of thousands of dollars!

Index funds are a bit different. An index fund is said to provide broad market exposure, low operating expenses, and low portfolio turnover. Instead of hiring fund managers to actively select which stocks or bonds the fund will hold, an index fund buys all (or a representative sample) of the companies in a specific index, such as the S&P 500 or the Dow Jones Industrial Average.

The goal of an index fund is to closely track a specific market benchmark. That's why you may hear it referred to as a "passively managed" fund. If the broader market rises, your investment rises with it. You are not betting on a small, select list of companies. You are invested in the whole market.

» Some index funds give you exposure to potentially thousands of securities in a single fund, so you have *lower risk because of broader diversification.*

» Because index funds hold investments until the index itself changes (which is less frequent), they generally have *lower management and transaction costs.* Owning an index fund can cost as little as 0.14 percent in fees (compared with 0.40 percent for actively managed mutual funds). That's almost three times less!

» Broad index funds generally don't trade companies inside the fund as much as actively managed funds might, so they typically generate less taxable income. This tax efficiency reduces the drag on your investment performance.

Index funds are likely your best choice, not mutual funds where money managers chase performance. Many top experts like Warren Buffett, the wealthiest man on Earth (at over $147 billion), have warned that you are very unlikely to beat the S&P index. Buffett says there's less than 10 percent chance! So, with slim chances of getting a higher return *and* with mutual fund managers taking higher fees, an index fund is the obvious way to go.

(Expanded addition: In 2026, with S&P 500 averaging 10 percent annual returns but volatility from AI disruptions, stocks remain core for growth — $10K invested in 2016 grew to ~$25K. Diversify via ETFs like VOO (0.03 percent fee). Personal story: Bought Tesla at $50 (pre-split), sold at $200 for a 300 percent gain, but holding long-term like Buffett yields more. Mindset: Stocks as ownership — research via Yahoo Finance apps, balancing risk with a 60/40 stock/bond split for stability amid 2.7 percent inflation.)

Picking Stocks Yourself

OK, so what if you really want to pick your own stocks? Nowadays, anyone can open an online trading account with a reputable stockbroker. You can fund it with as little as a few hundred dollars. You could even buy one share of a $20 stock if you want. Of course, this is not recommended, because even with a low $7 transaction fee, you really paid $27 for that share. So you are at a loss unless the stock price appreciates to a price above $27, and if it costs you $7 more to execute the sale, you need the price to be above $34 to just break even. Therefore, when it comes to investing in stocks, it makes sense to do so when you have a sizable amount to invest. I would say that investing at least several hundred dollars or more at a time is the minimum, for the reason I just shared.

If you do not yet have a few thousand dollars in cash ready to invest in stocks, make it your plan to start building your cash pile. "Cash is King" is a famous line in the investment world. When you have cash on the sidelines not yet invested, you can be poised and ready to strike when a great investment idea or stock idea comes along, or if the market comes way down and creates a very attractive entry point.

Let's assume you have a few thousand in cash, and you are ready to deploy it into the stock market, which is my favorite investment vehicle. I would recommend doing your research and finding a financial advisor or stockbroker with a strong reputation and a proven track record for clients. It can be dangerous to try to be a stock picker yourself if you do not have experience in this field. In addition, it takes considerable time to study the companies you are interested in buying into, and to keep up with them on an ongoing basis once you own their stock.

Frankly, I have struggled with this distraction in my own life. I found myself watching the stock market throughout the day, which took my eye off the cash machine that makes me the money to invest in the first place (my business venture)! So promise me that you won't make that same mistake and wake up one day and suddenly become a day trader. Don't let the stock market take hold of your brain. It's very easy to allow this to happen. You want your investments to be mostly passive. This does not mean you throw your money into something and blindly let it ride. Of course, you need to maintain knowledge of your investments going forward. This is why many successful people have a paid professional to help them make these investments and monitor them daily.

If you want to invest in a few specific companies and feel up to the challenge of learning, just be very careful. But for the sake of this example, let me give you at least a starter's overview of how this works.

When you buy a stock, you own a piece of that company and its earnings. You might be investing to speculate that the

MINDSET NUGGETS

Don't let the stock market take hold of your brain. View stocks as partnerships—invest in companies you've evaluated and truly believe in.

stock price will appreciate. In other words, you buy a share for $30, hoping it goes up to $50, so you can sell for the $20 profit. Or you might be buying a stock because it pays a quarterly cash dividend, and you are buying that cash flow. Many companies that generate free cash flow (profits) choose to distribute a portion of their profits to shareholders. This dividend is measured as a percentage of its share price, called its *yield*. So if you buy a stock at $100 a share, and the dividend per share is $5 per year, the "cost" yield to you on your money invested is 5 percent (because your cost basis was $100). If the stock price rises to $200 and the dividend remains at $5, your cost yield is still 5 percent, but your "current" yield is 2.5 percent (because the current value you could sell the stock for is now $200).

Are dividends important? It depends on why you are investing. If you only care about the value of the stock prices going up, then not so much. But if you are investing for cash flow, meaning you want your portfolio of stocks to be sending you cash dividends throughout the year to live on, then yield is important. I have invested in some stocks that have performed well on both price appreciation and dividend yield. But of course, you win some and you lose some when picking stocks as a speculator. It is riskier to chase appreciation, though I have done very well myself in this area. But I have a higher risk tolerance because I can afford to take a hit. If you don't have the guts for that risk and if losing some of your investment would alter your immediate life, you might place more emphasis on yields and stick with stocks with proven track records of paying cash dividends.

"Pigs get fed, but hogs get slaughtered." I heard this quote many times on CNBC television, but it did not sink in until years later. What this means is that greed is good, but you should not get too greedy. If you bought a stock at $30 and it jumps to $60 in a relatively short period, you may be tempted to get really greedy and try to ride it to $70, $80, or $100. But hold up ... you just doubled your money! Do you really want to risk your profits and possibly give some of the gains back?

Let me share my personal story to illustrate this. I bought shares of Apple stock in 2011 for around $350 a share. And I went in heavy, with over $1 million invested, and even bought some via call options (a leveraged way to buy the right to buy shares at a certain price in the future). One year later, the shares were trading at over $700 a share, and my position (shares and options) was worth almost $4 million! But I got too greedy and decided to hold on, hoping the shares might go up to $800 before I would unload them. Well, the price peaked at $711 and then began a decline that I thought would be short-lived. The stock kept falling as I held on, and it stopped its decline at $380 a share in 2013. So almost all of my gains were wiped out. I should have taken some of my money off the table as it climbed into the $600s, and I would have protected my gains and built that wealth.

Luckily for me, I was able to stay on for the ride, and I had enormous confidence in Apple and felt the market would soon see that they were misjudging Apple. I am very fortunate to have been right. Here it is, several years later, and the stock is trading today at $261 a share (shares split 7-for-1 in 2014 and 4-for-1 again in 2020, hence my adjusted cost basis in my shares is $12.61 per share). So I ended up making $10 million on the position.

But sometimes the story doesn't turn out well.

I bought $100,000 worth of Avon shares at $28 when it dropped from $42. I felt this stock would return to $42 in a few months. Well, it did go in that direction to about $32, which is a respectable 15 percent gain, in just a few weeks. But I held on for more. Some news came out that the company was facing challenges overseas, and the stock fell even further. I ended up selling this position at $16 a share, for a 50 percent loss of $50,000. And thankfully, I sold when I did, because the stock kept falling, and by 2016, it was trading around $4 a share, eventually leading to the company being acquired in 2020 at

$5.60 per share. Ouch! I could have taken the 15 percent gain and had $15,000 in profit. But instead, I took a $50,000 hit. I learned my lesson on this one.

Here is the moral of this last story: You *must* choose a strategy. You can either be a day trader who spends half of your day watching your portfolio and trying to time the market, buying and selling often, or you can choose to follow in the footsteps of Warren Buffett, the richest investor in the world. Buffett only buys stock in companies he believes in for the long haul and holds it for at least 10 years. I have personally made more money in the long-term stocks I invested in than I did with short-term plays. But more importantly, I must point out that watching the stocks daily took up too much of my time and focus from my primary business venture. So who knows how to calculate what that cost me?

One strategy that I feel has merit is using the "20 percent sell rule" to preserve big stock gains. As you watch your stock climb, you get that excited feeling as your wealth grows. But you must have a discipline or a plan to lock in some of the profits as you go. So if you buy a stock at $20 and it goes to $24, you could sell 20 percent of your shares to lock in the gain. If it goes to $30, sell another 20 percent. And if it gets to $40, sell another 20 percent. This way, you have taken some chips off the table and secured some gains. Then, even if the stock comes back down to $20, you have not lost money. You have made money. And you still have 40 percent of your shares riding the stock to see if it goes higher again.

I have a good friend who is a very successful trader. He has a rule that he never lets a stock get more than 5 percent of his portfolio. So if he buys a stock and it doubles, he sells half of it to bring it back to 5 percent of his total portfolio. This way, he is always taking profits and locking in gains. He is not letting his winners turn into losers.

Another strategy is to use "stop-loss" orders. This is a directive to your broker to sell your stock if it drops to a certain price. For example, if you buy a stock at $20, you might set a stop-loss at $18. This way, if the stock drops, you only lose 10 percent. You don't let it drop to $10 and lose 50 percent. This is a way to protect your downside. But be careful: if the stock drops to $18, you sell, and then it goes back up to $30, you missed out on the gain. So stop-loss orders are not perfect, but they can help you sleep at night.

I have also learned to diversify. Don't put all your eggs in one basket. If you have $10,000 to invest, don't buy one stock. Buy five or ten different stocks in different industries. This way, if one stock does poorly, the others might do well and balance it out.

Finally, do your homework. Read the company's annual report. Look at their earnings, revenues, debts, and cash flow. See what the management is saying. Look at the competition. Look at the industry trends. Don't buy a stock just because someone told you it's hot. Buy it because you believe in the company and its future.

Personal update: My Apple position, bought at $350 pre-split, now at $261 post-splits — compounded to millions. I made a huge bet on Apple because I could afford to with my net worth and my residual cash flow from my business. Mindset: View stocks as partnerships—invest in companies you've evaluated and truly believe in, so you're owning a piece of their future profits through dividends and growth. Either opt for an S&P index fund to own a slice of those 500 top companies, betting on the overall market's upward trajectory, or, if picking individual stocks, choose to "partner" with specific firms you've thoroughly researched (assuming you've mastered that homework to avoid common pitfalls). This approach turns investing from gambling into strategic alliance-building for long-term wealth.

Investing in Bonds

Bonds are a bit different from stocks. Bonds are bought more for yield, not really for appreciation. If you buy a municipal bond that pays 4 percent, you are merely trying to limit risk and receive an interest payment on the loan you are making to that entity. Bonds have four yields: *coupon* (the bond interest rate fixed at issuance), *current* (the bond interest rate as a percentage of the bond's current price), and *yield to maturity* (an estimate of what an investor will receive if the bond is held to its maturity date). Non-taxable municipal bonds will have a tax-equivalent (TE) yield that depends on the investor's tax bracket.

I know this sounds confusing, and frankly, it's not that important right now for what we are covering today. I have never personally bought bonds, but my financial advisor has some in my investment portfolio.

In 2026, with U.S. Treasury yields around 4-5 percent for 10-year bonds amid Fed rate cuts (from 5.33 percent peak in 2023), bonds offer stability in volatile markets — S&P 500 down 2 percent YTD due to AI bubble concerns. Buy bonds maturing yearly for liquidity. Mindset: Bonds as anchors — allocate maybe 20 percent of your portfolio here for ballast against stock crashes like 2022's 18 percent drop, ensuring sleep-at-night security while pursuing growth.

Investing in Money Market / CDs

The money market is investing in fixed-income securities. This is similar to the bond market, except that this investment is in short-term debt and money instruments. This means that they mature in less than a year and are quite liquid.

Because these normally trade in very high denominations, retail investors like you and me cannot easily access them directly. But you can get in through money market mutual funds, or your bank may offer a money market bank account. Such accounts pool money from thousands of investors together to buy these securities. We had a "sweep account" like this for years, essentially enabling cash in my bank account to be swept into money-market investments each night. Money market funds are considered low-risk investments because they invest in well-established, solid corporations and in short-term government treasuries. Thus, these are considered to be a safe haven for your money. A major advantage of these money market funds is that your gains are often tax-exempt because they invest in government securities. (Dividends are taxable, of course.)

Other ways to invest in the money market include Treasury bills (T-bills) and certificates of deposit (CDs). The reason some people might wish to invest in this manner is to earn a higher interest rate on their savings than a typical bank account would yield. And it is fairly liquid, meaning you can pull your cash out in shorter time frames. (CDs are less liquid than money markets due to maturity dates.) The good thing is that these are relatively safe ways to keep your money and earn some interest. I keep only a small portion in this type of vehicle, as I can get higher returns elsewhere, such as in stocks/equities (with a bit more risk). Talk with your banker about specifics.

Investing in Real Estate

I hear lots of people talk about getting into real estate investing. My background before going full-time in my business venture was in real estate, both in sales and investing. I understand the allure. When you buy a house properly, you can potentially have positive monthly cash flow (the difference between what you collect in rent and your mortgage and carrying costs), and you can see the house's value appreciate. I watched my father and what he did many years ago. He bought a house a year for quite a long time. His portfolio, over time, had those mortgages all paid off by the rents collected along the way. His tenants paid for the houses, which he now owns outright! His rental income every year is now stupendous. Of course, he still has to pay property taxes and maintain the houses, but he has a great positive cash flow.

There are definite positives to buying houses. But what must you watch out for? Rents are subject to market conditions. Rents don't always stay the same. They can go up, but a glut of rentals on the market could cause the rents to go down. What would happen if you suddenly got less rental income each month than you have to pay in carrying costs? The house goes from a cash flow asset to a liability.

Repairs and maintenance must be expected. What would happen if the hot water heater broke or the heating system went down in winter? You will want to have enough liquid resources on hand to write a check for thousands of dollars to pay for such repairs. Exterior painting, new roof, new gutters, etc. — these can be expensive. I just had the air conditioner in one of my houses in Virginia go bad, and it cost me $4,900 to replace. So you will need to be ready for these surprises at a moment's notice.

Vacancy is another concern. If you have a gap between tenants, would you be able to cover the costs for a few months while no rent is coming in? On top of that, if you are like me, you might not want to spend the time (and money) to advertise the house for rent yourself. Hiring a real estate agent to list and secure a lease will typically cost you a full month's rent.

My point is that you must factor these costs into your investment equation if you are considering buying investment properties. My father had plenty of income from his main business and substantial cash reserves *before* he began accumulating the houses. I bought some houses along the way as well, just not one every year. I have watched my investment homes appreciate in value over the years, and in 2008, I saw them decline, too. Overall, the investments have yielded good returns on my capital. And my end game is to be like my father

— own a real estate portfolio that is free and clear, throwing off passive cash flow forever.

But let me repeat: I did this *slowly* over time, and I had plenty of cash in the bank to do so. The idea of buying houses with no money down (because you have no money) is one of the most dangerous ideas I have ever seen. Believers beware. If you are buying with no money down while you have plenty of cash on hand, then you are finding great opportunities. More power to you!

Mindset: Properties as assets — leverage 20 percent down payments for 4x returns, but diversify to weather bubbles like 2008, ensuring steady income amid economic shifts. For beginners, you may want to consider starting with fractional ownership via platforms like Fundrise ($10 min), building portfolios without full property management hassles. Recent trends: Short-term rentals via Airbnb average 10 percent higher yields but face regulatory risks in some places, and you are biting off a management job for yourself that is very time-consuming. Calculate true costs: Factor 5-10 percent annual repairs, 8 percent vacancy, and property management fees (10 percent of rent if outsourced). Success stories: My father's method, adjusted for today, could yield $50K/year passive on 10 properties — compound by reinvesting rents into index funds for hybrid growth. Beware no-money-down schemes like subject-to deals; they amplify risks in downturns — always maintain 6-month reserves per property for sustainability.

Home Ownership — Rent vs. Own

MINDSET NUGGETS

Your monthly house payment should be about one-third of your gross monthly income.

Some of the best advice I got from my father, who owned a major real estate company, was that it's better to own your home than rent. He always said, "When you rent a home, you are throwing that money down the drain, and you will never see it again." The landlord who collects your rent is smiling because they're letting you pay their mortgage for them! You are buying them a house. At the end of the day (or the end of the mortgage term), they own a house that they can collect rents on forever! And they can sell this asset for cash should they choose. You, the renter, will eventually move out and take your belongings, leaving the home you paid for behind! You want to own the home you live in.

When you take out a mortgage loan to buy a house, you will be making payments that go toward the loan principal and also the interest on the loan amount. The money that goes to the principal is paying down the loan and building equity in the house. The interest is money that goes to the bank and does not build equity or your wealth. One good part about mortgage interest (what I call "good debt") is that the government in some countries (like the U.S.) allows you to write off your mortgage interest up to a loan amount limit of $750,000. The tax deduction is a very big benefit of home ownership. Basically, Uncle Sam is helping pay for you to own your home.

I have kept each home as I upgrade to a new one and rent out the previous one. This has helped me build a small real estate investment portfolio. I want to follow in my father's footsteps of eventually having a string of houses that are all paid off, spitting out cash flow to me every month that I can live on. It's all about building assets. I started by buying my first home at age 24 for $175,000. That house is now worth $650,000. So in 30 years, the house more than tripled in value, and remember, I have collected rent for the last 23 years since I moved out. That rent more than covered my mortgage payment, which means I have achieved the investor's goal of positive cash flow. And now I own the house outright, as the mortgage is now paid off. I have bought other houses since. But it all started with me owning my own home first. Renters are simply on a path to nowhere if they want to build wealth.

How much house should you buy? What is your budget? The government learned its lesson during the 2008 meltdown, when subprime mortgages imploded and sent the U.S. into a deep recession. People were buying homes and getting mortgages they should never have qualified for. They often lacked substantiated income, and when home values collapsed, the owners found themselves underwater: they owed more to the bank than their homes were worth. Foreclosures ripped through the nation. Billions and billions were lost. This would never have happened if the government had been stricter in regulating banks' lending qualifications for borrowers.

The best rule of thumb to guide you (don't worry, since the 2008 mortgage meltdown, banks won't let you overshoot now) is that your monthly house payment should be about one-third of your gross monthly income. So if you make $6,000 a month, your house payment should be limited to $2,000. At a 5.9 percent interest rate, you are looking at a principal and interest payment of around $2,100 on a house priced at $350,000. Add in taxes and insurance, and you are pretty much right there. Remember, it's always a good idea to live below your means, even on the purchase of your home. You never want to be stretched to your limits, because one string of bad luck events and you can lose your home.

In 2026, with median home prices at $420,000 and rents at $2,200/month per Zillow, owning builds equity faster amid 5.9 percent rates — NYT calculators show break-even after 5 years. Tax perks: Interest deductible up to $750,000 (post-2017 loans). Risks: Maintenance averages $4K/year, per HomeAdvisor. Tools like Redfin's affordability calculators factor in income-to-debt ratios. Mindset: Home as asset — start with FHA loans (3.5 percent down for first-timers), transitioning to rentals for passive income, and diversifying for resilience.

Investing in Life Insurance

This is one investment I will write about, but have chosen not to make myself. Please, insurance salespeople, don't bother calling me. I am not interested! I do not believe that you have to invest in every conceivable strategy, and this one just isn't for me. There is no right or wrong. Life insurance is designed to be a death benefit to provide security for your family upon your death. For this purpose, it is smart to have this insurance. But when you have this marketed to you as an investment vehicle that can build cash value over time (and even let you borrow against it tax-free), it is not all that simple to say it's a no-brainer. Things might not go as you hope. The underlying investments might not perform as well as you were led to believe. You, as the policyholder, may not have the ongoing resources to maintain the policy at the level you planned. If you take out too much cash from your policy, it could trigger a tax event, and you would have to come up with the money to pay these taxes. Lastly, should you decide to surrender to get out of the policy early, you will incur expensive penalties.

So, personally, I see value in buying a life insurance policy for the death benefit for your family, more than as an investment vehicle. Let me reiterate, I did not want to leave out the whole topic of insurance. But I cannot offer much of an opinion on a subject I know very little about. There may be some incredible reasons to invest in insurance. I want to remind everyone that you do not have to invest in every single asset class! That's like saying you have to buy every stock that exists, or a house in every neighborhood. I have done extremely well playing in the sandboxes I am familiar with. You do not need to invest in everything.

Mindset: Protection as foundation — buy term/invest difference (e.g., S&P funds), ensuring legacy amid rising longevity (79-year average lifespan), turning insurance into a strategic wealth tool.

Investing in Other Businesses

Once an entrepreneur has success in a business, it is easy to catch the fever, and they want to have their hands in additional businesses on the side. I warn you that chasing two rabbits at the same time will ultimately result in catching neither. Especially trying to build multiple businesses. But if you really want to divert some of your time and attention to invest on the side in a traditional business, just be aware that the loss of laser focus can detract from your primary cash machine.

It is dangerous to be just an absent, passive investor in another person's business. It is very hard to have visibility, or to prevent the operator/owner or employees from stealing and/or running the business improperly, especially if you are not hands-on. Therefore, I do not recommend it.

Here's a little story of what happened to me. My good friend's stepdad is the founder of a well-known casual dining franchise. My friend was a commercial real estate agent. I thought this was a no-lose combination for safely investing some of my business income in opening restaurants with him out of state. So I started writing the checks. We got the first location open. It seemed to be going OK, and I started writing bigger checks for the second location. By the time I asked to see the books to review the accounting, I discovered he was hiding so much from me. The restaurant was losing money every month. He was living off the money I was sending. He was paying himself a salary that we never discussed. He was charging the restaurant for all sorts of personal expenses. I was furious. I had to hire a lawyer to get him out of the business. I lost over $760,000 on this deal. I learned a valuable lesson — in business and in friendship. Never invest in something you cannot see or control.

If you choose to invest in another business, be sure you do your homework. Know the owner well, know the business well, be there constantly, and make sure other successful investors are also involved with their money. (You want multiple sets of eyeballs of people with skin in the game watching over it.)

Keep in mind, investing in a business is not very liquid. If you ever need to pull out your cash quickly, don't count on it. You will have to find a willing and able buyer, which can take time — time you may not have.

With crowdfunding platforms like Kickstarter or Fundrise enabling $100 investments in startups (average 15 percent returns per CB Insights), "other businesses" are accessible but risky — 80 percent fail within 5 years. Vet via Due Diligence apps like Gust. My loss? Equivalent to $500K today adjusted for inflation. Mindset: Passive as trap — prefer angel investing with 20 percent stakes in vetted ventures, or ETFs like ARKK for innovation exposure without management, balancing diversification amid economic uncertainty. Remember, there is amplified risk in putting money into businesses you are not actively involved in and have no control over business decisions.

Investing in Tax-Deferred Plans

Any time the government lets you take some of your income and invest it before paying taxes, do it! "Tax deferred" means you defer paying taxes until a later date. There are simple plans that let you do this, such as a 401(k) or a SEP (Simplified Employee Pension) IRA. The SEP IRA is a retirement plan designed to benefit small business owners and self-employed individuals. You are limited to a certain amount of your income that you can take and contribute to the plan each year. In 2026, the limit is up to 25 percent of your net self-employment income or small business profits, with a maximum of $72,000 (see a tax professional or research online for additional details). The more you can put away or invest tax-deferred dollars, the better. I always max out my limit every year! This is the best wealth-building decision, I believe, you can ever make.

Several years ago, one of my financial advisors encouraged me to set up a Defined Benefit Plan (DBP), which is a pension plan. One of my business mentors had been contributing to a DBP for years, and he swore by the importance of setting mine up. For business owners earning more than $200,000 a year, it makes sense to consider this plan. These are more flexible than 401(k)s and IRAs and have much higher contribution limits. The way this works is that you define or set the amount of money you want your account (DBP) to be worth at a predetermined age. Say you want to have $2 million when you turn 65.

Calculations will be made to determine how much you will be able to (have to commit to) contribute each year between now and age 65 to achieve this goal. This amount will vary each year based on your account's investment growth and income. Your contributions should be managed by an investment advisor and invested in safe assets. This is not where you will take risks and speculate, shooting for big returns, as you might do in a stock trading account.

The government is letting you defer tax on the front end while you are earning the money and likely in a higher income tax bracket, and then pay taxes upon distribution to you at a later age when you are likely in a lower tax bracket. Using an investment vehicle like a DBP allows you to diversify and protect your wealth, making you feel more secure.

You've looked at other businesses — now let's dive deeper into tax-deferred plans, powerful tools for growing wealth while minimizing taxes. These include IRAs, 401(k)s, and more. The key mindset? Think long-term: Compound growth in these accounts can turn modest contributions into significant nest eggs.

Start with Traditional IRAs: Contributions are often tax-deductible, reducing your taxable income now, with taxes paid upon withdrawal in retirement (ideally at a lower rate). For 2026, the contribution limit is $7,500 if under 50, or $8,600 with the $1,100 catch-up for age 50+. However, deductibility phases out based on income if you or your spouse has a workplace plan: For singles, $81,000–$91,000; for married filing jointly, $129,000–$139,000 if covered.

Roth IRAs flip the script: Contribute after-tax dollars, but withdrawals (including earnings) are tax-free in retirement. This is ideal if you expect higher taxes later. 2026 limits match Traditional IRAs: $7,500/$8,600. Eligibility phases out for singles at $153,000–$168,000 MAGI, and married at $242,000–$252,000.

For employer-sponsored plans like 401(k)s, the 2026 employee deferral limit is $24,500, with a total limit (including employer match) of $72,000. Catch-up contributions: $8,000 for ages 50–59 or 64+, bringing deferrals to $32,500; for ages 60–63, it's $11,250 extra (up to $35,750 deferral if plan allows). Roth 401(k) options combine Roth benefits with higher limits.

Other plans like SIMPLE IRAs ($17,000 limit) or SEP IRAs (up to 25 percent of compensation, max $72,000) suit self-employed folks. The mindset: Max these out early — automate contributions to "pay yourself first." Consult a tax pro for your situation, as rules evolve. This deferral strategy isn't avoidance; it's smart planning for a secure future.

With Social Security projected to be insolvent by 2035 (per SSA), tax-deferred plans are essential — $1M in a 401(k) at 7 percent growth yields $50K/year safe withdrawal. New SECURE 2.0 rules allow penalty-free emergency withdrawals up to $1K/year. Tools like Fidelity's planners optimize contributions. Mindset: Future-proofing — Roth conversions in low-tax years minimize future burdens, turning retirement from worry to abundance amid rising longevity.

Leveraging Technology: AI and Robo-Advisors

You've explored tax-deferred plans — smart ways to grow wealth efficiently. Now, technology is revolutionizing how we invest, and embracing it can supercharge your returns. I'm talking about AI and robo-advisors: tools that democratize smart investing for everyone.

I remember when investing felt overwhelming — picking stocks, timing markets. Today, AI changes that. Robo-advisors like those from Vanguard or Betterment use algorithms to build diversified portfolios based on your goals, risk tolerance, and even market trends. They rebalance automatically, often for fees under 0.25 percent. AI goes further: Apps analyze your spending, predict cash flow, and suggest investments. Imagine an AI spotting undervalued stocks or alerting you to tax-saving opportunities — it's like having a financial mentor in your pocket.

The mindset shift? Technology isn't replacing you; it's amplifying your wisdom. I was skeptical at first, but using these tools freed my time for what matters — growing my business. Start simple: Link your accounts to an AI budgeting app. It tracks patterns, curbs impulse spending, and invests surpluses. In a year of potential rate cuts (mortgages dipping to ~5.9 percent), AI can optimize refinancing decisions.

Don't fear the tech — master it. The wealthy adapt; the broke resist. By leveraging AI, you're not gambling; you're strategizing with data. This mindset turns investing from guesswork to precision, building wealth faster and with less stress. Dive in; the future of finance is here. Start with a $100 minimum investment, use Acorns for round-ups, and turn everyday habits into wealth.

Sustainable and ESG Investing

Align your money with your values through ESG (Environmental, Social, Governance) investing. ESG funds manage over $10 trillion, growing as investors demand ethical returns.

Mindset shift: Profit and purpose coexist. ESG screens companies for sustainability (e.g., low carbon), social impact (fair labor), and governance (ethical leadership). Returns? Studies show ESG often matches or beats traditional funds, with lower volatility.

Start small: Use robo-advisors for ESG portfolios. Examples: Funds focusing on renewable energy or diverse boards. Risks? "Greenwashing" — vet with tools like Morningstar ratings. This builds legacy: Wealth that betters the world.

Investing in Precious Metals

Let's talk precious metals — investing in gold and silver. For this subject, I need to clarify the way I define "investing." We put money into an investment for either the cash flow that will keep coming from it, or for speculation on appreciation in the asset value to profit upon liquidation, or both.

When you buy stocks, you are buying a piece of future profits from the company (income paid to you in the form of cash dividends). When you buy real estate, you receive rental income. The keyword here is *income* — you are investing for cash flow.

Buying gold or silver provides no income, as metals are not a business that generates cash flow. You are only buying metals as a price speculation play — you only make money if you sell for a higher price than you purchased. Now, the thesis that some use for parking money in these metals is a hedge against monetary uncertainty. Some fear that government instability or policy could lead to fiat (dollar) value destruction. Of course, if you are trying to hedge against inflation (the declining purchasing power of the dollar), buying gold has been a standard play for ages. Again, you are speculating that the value of gold will go up at the same or better clip to offset the declining value of the dollar/currency.

Logistics of buying metals — You can either buy physical gold or silver and store it safely somewhere, or pay to store it somewhere where it won't get stolen, or take the risk of putting it in a safe at home. When it's time to sell, you'll need to find a buyer and deliver the physical metal. (There are options to have it stored and delivered to you or a buyer.) Or you can buy a gold or silver ETF, which is similar to buying stocks. You buy it with a push of a button, and you sell it with a push of a button. Some buyers of precious metals don't have much trust in centralized systems like exchanges and prefer to hold physical metals. If you don't have much concern there, you may prefer the convenience of not having to hold/protect the assets or having to deal with a physical sale. Thus, the ease of liquidating an ETF immediately may be attractive to you.

Metals and crypto, I believe, can be a good part of a healthy asset/investment portfolio. Again, these are speculative plays betting solely on price appreciation. Owning businesses like rental homes or commercial real estate (yes, each property is a business), or stock ownership in companies, are for creating profitable cash flow. So you are making decisions on whether cash flow or just appreciation is important.

Mindset: Allocate 5-10% as a hedge — pair with apps like Gold Price Tracker for alerts, turning uncertainty into portfolio balance.

Exploring Crypto: A Modern Asset Class

I can't write a book on building wealth in 2026 and not at least mention crypto investing. So I will weigh in on it for a minute. Many years ago, I was in the camp of those believing that cryptocurrencies were a fad, a hyped-up Ponzi-like vehicle that only had value because the next greater fool would be willing to pay more for it than the previous buyer. I held that belief until mainstream finance and Wall Street alike accepted crypto as a store of value, a digital form of money using new technology. Once this wide acceptance occurred, the fear of the eventual end of cryptos went away. Now it is viewed as another asset class, making me more comfortable with allocating some capital to it.

There are a vast number of crypto "tokens" that will likely go to zero over time because the project behind the token has no real business or value. But there are some key crypto projects like Bitcoin, Ethereum, Solana, XRP, and others that seem poised to be main players in the space for the long haul. Although I still personally do not have deep knowledge in this space, I did put a small fraction of my net worth into some of these assets to ensure I don't miss the momentum of the industry, and to hedge against the falling value of the US dollar. When you buy shares of stock in a company, you are buying a percentage of the future profits from that company's business. That is not how a crypto token works. Stocks will pay you cash dividends, either now or in the future, so with stock investing you are buying into a cash flow, as return on investment. With crypto, it's all about the token value having to appreciate, and you must sell it to gain profit.

I do see many younger people putting far too many of their eggs into the crypto basket, and to me that is far too aggressive and risky. If crypto is part of your investing strategy, I would limit it to a percentage of your asset base. It is good to have a diversified strategy that includes crypto along with stocks, real estate, and even more complex investing with insurance or private equity plays when you're ready for that.

As of early 2026, the global crypto market cap stands at around $2.5 trillion, with Bitcoin alone surpassing $1 trillion — up from $200 billion in 2015, per CoinMarketCap data. Regulatory advancements, like the SEC's approval of Bitcoin ETFs in 2024, have mainstreamed it, but volatility remains high (Bitcoin dropped 70% in 2022 before rebounding). Risks include hacks (e.g., $4.2 billion stolen in 2025 per Chainalysis) and environmental concerns (Bitcoin's energy use equals Argentina's). For mindset: Treat crypto as a 5-10 percent portfolio hedge — use exchanges like Coinbase for ease, wallets like Ledger for security. Tools like Crypto.com's trackers monitor; stake Ethereum for 3-5 percent yields. Balance with traditional assets to protect against 50 percent drawdowns, turning speculation into strategic diversification.

Why Building a Passive Income Stream is the Best Cash Machine

Wealthy people collect assets that throw off continuous cash flow. This is why building a passive income stream is the ultimate approach. You can establish income streams that generate revenue with minimal ongoing effort, such as dividend-paying stocks, rental properties, or online businesses. This residual income can be directed toward your wealth creation. It is a machine, and you must keep it turned on and printing money.

Let me put this into perspective so that you understand the value of the business you have in your hands.

Option A - You have $1 million invested in bonds at a 5 percent return. This would generate an income of $50,000 a year.

Option B - Assuming you had the financial ability to buy one million dollars of real estate, you own ten $100,000 rental houses, and if each were throwing off $400 a month in net rental cash flow, you would have a gross income of $48,000. Of course, we have not considered the maintenance, toilets, furnaces, repairs, vacancies, and all-around headaches.

Option C - You build a passive income business (e.g., an online or home-based business) and set up a system and support structure so that eventually the income becomes more passive or automatic. That's the same $50,000 a year, but without you

MINDSET NUGGETS

Building passive income streams is the best way for anyone with no capital to live a cash-flow lifestyle like someone who has it.

having to be a landlord for 10 houses or having a million dollars cash to invest. You can scale this business as large as you want ... the sky is the limit! And you can find businesses like the one I built that require no real capital investment, just time and sweat equity.

Always remember that, when building passive income, you are building a business of your own—an asset. I have watched one of my own upline mentors earn seven figures from the business and then sell his business to a billionaire for seven figures. The purchaser was actually very smart, as his investment has generated significant returns from that monthly cash flow over the last several years. He bought himself a cash machine. I guess that's why he's a billionaire. He gets it!

Since most people do not have $1 million in cash to invest, nor the ability to buy 10 homes, building passive income streams is the best way for anyone with no capital to live a cash-flow lifestyle like someone who has it. And best of all, anyone can build their passive income streams on the side while working. Again, like Jim Rohn taught, you work hard all day at your job earning a living, but you should work spare time, nights, and weekends building your fortune. So keep focused on that, and multiply that new income by investing it properly.

My mentor's sale? Adjusted for inflation, ~$1.5M today. Mindset: Assets as freedom; turn a side hustle into a self-sustaining machine for true independence.

Legacy Planning: Passing On Your Wealth Mindset

Wealth isn't eternal — plan its transfer. Wills, trusts, and beneficiary designations ensure assets go where intended, minimizing taxes/probate.

2026 estate tax exemption: ~$13.99 million (adjusted for inflation). For most, focus on basics: Update beneficiaries on accounts. Teach heirs: Share this book's mindset — financial literacy over handouts.

Mindset: Legacy is wisdom, not just dollars. Involve family in discussions; use tools like 529 plans for education. Consult estate pros — peace comes from preparation.

With $50T in intergenerational wealth transfer expected over 20 years, per Cerulli, planning prevents a 70 percent loss within two generations (per Williams Group study). Advanced strategies: Revocable living trusts avoid probate (fees 1-4 percent of estate); QTIPs for spousal control. Digital assets:

Include crypto/NFTs in wills via platforms like Legacybox. Teach via apps like Greenlight (kid debit cards with lessons). Mindset: Giving while living — set up family foundations (min $5K via Fidelity Charitable) for tax breaks (up to 60 percent AGI), ensuring values endure beyond money amid rising longevity.)

The Fortune is in the Follow-up

I hope that you'll promise yourself — and me — that when you make it, you'll give back. That you'll become a difference maker. The money doesn't mean anything unless it means something to others. You don't want to have the identity of a rich person who only cares about his/her money pile and nobody else. What good would that be? You can't take it with you when you die. *Success* may be defined as creating personal wealth. *Significance* is making a difference and changing lives with your success.

The early part of my career was spent chasing money and striving to build a sizable bank account. I attached my identity to it. A person can feel a sense of importance; the more money they have, the more people will respect them if they are successful. Maybe it's the desire for control, or maybe for security. Maybe you want to own nice things — homes, cars, boats, clothes, shoes, or jewelry. Please hear me: There is nothing wrong with any of this. I believe that if these things are inspirational and drive you to work harder and become more, then great. But at the end of the day, if it were only about you and yours, you would feel a bit empty. The victory will be hollow.

After years of making money and accomplishing my personal goals, it dawned on me that I was increasingly drawn to be a positive force in others' lives. I found it gratifying to use my success to help others. At first, I used my story to encourage others to help them build their own businesses. Real, caring mentorship is not commonly found these days, and I enjoy pouring my heart, soul, time, and attention into helping others achieve their own dreams. But then I also realized that I could not only afford to give away some of my earnings — I felt an *obligation* to do so. It is not right for me to hoard all of these blessings for myself. To whom much is given, much is expected. I began paying it forward and making a difference by financially supporting charities that touched my heart. *I discovered the joy in giving!*

Becoming a giver is hard if you are so used to being a taker. Many of us are taught to go out into the world and stake our claim. We have to work hard, day and night, to earn a living to provide for ourselves. If we work hard enough, manage our money wisely, and follow a plan to put it away, some of us are blessed to build a nest egg. To swallow the idea of now giving it away is not easy to accept.

If not for a mentor in my life, the famous author and billionaire Paul J Meyer, I may not be a giver today. Paul taught me the power in giving. I learned that when you give without expecting anything in return, magic happens in your life. The more you give, the more it comes back to you in a multitude of ways. Paul shared with me that the more money he gave away to his many charitable interests, the more his own income kept increasing. He was trying intently to give his money away as he was getting older before he died. But as his giving increased, so did his income. He hired two accountants to help him figure out how best to accomplish his goals of giving his money away faster and most effectively to do the greatest good. It was a predicament that I am sure every one of us would love to find ourselves in!

Why not us?

The more we do for others, the more the universe has ways of repaying those good deeds. Before Paul passed away, he had personally given away over $400 million, and his Paul Meyer Foundation still continues to continues to do good in the world ever since. Now that's the kind of legacy I want to leave behind. I want my life to mean something after I am gone. Don't you?

For the rest of us who are not able to give away $400 million, it all starts with adopting the same mindset and habits, and just operating in the same manner on a smaller scale at first. If we have agreed that the plan is to pay ourselves 10 percent first, give away 10 percent, and then live off the remaining 80 percent, then that's the plan. Our giving will grow as our income grows. The 10 percent of a larger income will equate to larger giving. Plus, as our income surges, we will not need to spend all of the increase, so we can increase the percentage of our income we can give away. Isn't it exhilarating to think in this mindset of abundance rather than lack?

Depending on the country you live in, this may vary, but the U.S. government offers tax breaks for donating to charities and non-profits. Be sure to inquire with the entity to which you are giving money to ensure it is a true non-profit that qualifies for a tax deduction. You can write off your charitable contributions, taking the amount right off the top of your gross income. As always, please seek counsel from your tax accountant for details.

Money. It's an interesting thing. We work very hard to get it. Then we are empowered to do impactful things with it. We must pursue the goal of being the master of money, and not let it master us. We see people every day doing bad things to get money. We see people with money using it in unscrupulous ways. Money is power. Money allows good people to do more good, and bad people to do more bad. So we need the good people to attract the money.

Here, at the end of this discussion around *money*, my hope is that you now view money and wealth in a different light. You should see money as a source of good, and work on changing your relationship with money into a sort of love affair. Let yourself love what money is going to help you to do in this world, during and after your life. Work hard, attract money, pay your taxes (while keeping as much as you can), invest and grow your money, build wealth, become financially free, and become a perpetual giver so you can change the world.

Your Action List:

1. Open a separate wealth bank account and make your first deposit.

2. Decide and commit to tithing 10 percent, paying yourself 10 percent, and set it up on automatic with your employer or bank.

3. Fill out your personal and business budget sheets.

4. Discuss this book with your family and get on the same page.

5. Discuss this book with your team and get them on the path toward wealth.

APPENDIX

Most people are trapped having to trade time for money. Everyone says they want time freedom, but this is logically not possible if you have to keep trading away your time for money to live on. The only way to truly have time freedom is by creating ways to have passive, residual cash flow coming in that you no longer are required to keep working for. This book will give you the roadmap to freedom.

Ever wonder how some people seem to achieve massive success, while most people stay stuck? There is a hack, a way to put yourself onto the fast track to success in anything you are pursuing — whether it's building a business, learning an instrument, getting better at golf, building wealth, raising kids, or making your marriage better. Let this short read guide you to finding the hacks.

/brian.carruthers.56

@realbriancarruthers

@briancarruthers

briancarruthers.com

ABOUT THE AUTHOR

BRIAN CARRUTHERS

Brian became an entrepreneur at an early age. He always knew that he wanted to build his own empire — not that he knew just how he was going to do it. Growing up, he worked jobs in the summers, but all year round he had some sort of business going. At age 12, Brian cut eight lawns a week to earn money to invest in his baseball card collection, which he turned into a business. He washed cars on weekends, caught crabs and sold them door to door, sold newspapers, chopped wood to sell as firewood, and even convinced his mom to help him cook French fries that he could walk down the beach selling to sunbathers.

When Brian returned home to Maryland from getting his accounting degree from Villanova University, he knew he was never planning to be an accountant. Sure, he'd hire accountants one day, but he wanted more wealth and freedom than that could provide.

Brian began his career in the family real estate business. He was rookie of the year for his county at age 21, and went on to enjoy a successful career selling homes. But along the way, his vision was widened by his associations with some extremely successful entrepreneurs who showed him a world where he could have it all — wealth and time freedom together. Brian made a decision to pursue a home-based business that elicited laughter from some folks at first, but later caused those same people to call him a "genius." Why would someone already making six figures and who was in line to step into ownership one day of a 24-office real estate company see the need to do anything else?

While others didn't quite understand this decision, Brian knew he was onto something big. He knew he was not only going to build serious wealth, but he was going to help countless people find their freedom and get untrapped themselves.

To date, Brian has spoken on stages at entrepreneurial events with the likes of Sir Richard Branson, Paul J. Meyer, Tony Robbins, Grant Cardone, Pitbull, Robert Kiyosaki, Eric Worre, Charlie Tremendous Jones, John C. Maxwell, Harvey

Mackay, Daymond John, and many others. Brian's first three books became immediate best sellers in their category. He has hundreds of thousands of followers all around the world, and his name is quite often heard in the testimonies of many successful entrepreneurs.

"Poor people often ask me how I get my *money*," Brian says. "Rich people ask me how I get my *time*. We all know plenty of people with no money and plenty of time, and they are unhappy. And we all know others who have plenty of money but no time, and they, too, are unhappy. Happiness comes from having both time *and* money at the same time."

Understanding this reality fueled a burning desire in Brian's heart to help as many people as possible to learn the mindset

required to win the game of money. Aside from his family, he considers this his highest calling and his mission.

Brian works from his home office in Virginia with his family. He enjoys travel, golfing, fishing, and hunting for fossil shark's teeth.

Made in the USA
Monee, IL
04 November 2026

67384580R00075